The Taste Guides

PIER FRANCESCO LISTRI

Art, cuisine, and nature in

TUSCANY

Itineraries of foods, views, and festas

BONECHI EDIZIONI "IL TURISMO" FIRENZE

© Copyright 1999 by Bonechi Edizioni
'Il Turismo' S.r.l.
Via dei Rustici, 5 – 50122 Firenze, Italy
Tel. (+39) 055 239-8224
Fax (+39) 055 216366
Email: barbara@bonechi.com
        bbonechi@data.it
http://www.bonechi.com

Photos: Archivio Bonechi Edizioni 'Il Turismo'
S.r.l.; Archivio Millevolte Firenze (Florence);
Giovanni Piscolla (Florence); Emanuele
Pellucci (Florence); Matteo Listri (Florence);
Nicola Grifoni (Florence); Bruno Giovannetti
(Carrara); Foto Dainelli (Volterra); Giuliano
Valdes (Pisa); Foto Lensini (Siena); Archivio
A.P.T. Arezzo; Archivio A.P.T. Leghorn;
Archivio A.P.T. "Abetone Pistoia Montagna
P.se"; Archivio A.P.T. "Montecatini
Valdinievole"
Photo Lucca: Cornelio Timpani Image
Edition Florence: Concessione S.M.A. no. 256
del 13/07/95

Translated by: Merry Orling

Coordinator: Barbara Bonechi
Editorial staff: Lorena Lazzari
Drawings: Claudia Baggiani
Artwork: Antonio Tassinari

Photolithography: Cartografica, Florence
Paste-up: Fotolito Immagine, Florence
Printed by: La Zincografica Fiorentina, Florence
ISBN 88-7204-397-2

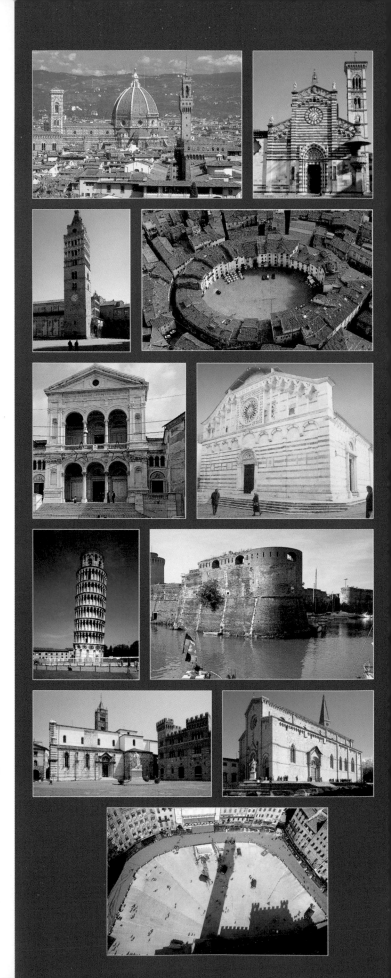

Many Tuscanies, one history

Tuscany is a land with many facets. It is a land of a myriad of panoramas, from the inland mountains (Apennines, Apuans, Amiata), valleys (Valdichiana, Lunigiana, Garfagnana, Mugello, Valdarno, Casentino), and plains, to the miles of coastal lands lying along the Tyrrhenian Sea. It is a land of striking contrasts, from the harmonious Chianti countryside between Siena and Florence to the untamed vistas of the Balze of Volterra, Crete of Siena, Colline Metallifere, and the Maremma, in whose forestlands roam wild animals, including wolves (rare) and boar, hares, foxes (numerous).

Tuscany vaunts the world's highest concentration of art masterpieces. Its splendid artisan tradition derives from the innate Tuscan talent for fashioning gold, silver, precious and semiprecious stones, leather, wood, straw, wrought-iron, marble, stone into marvelous objects. Still today, the big cities and the small towns, are dotted with the botteghe of the corniciai (frame makers), bronzisti (bronzesmiths), doratori (gilders), and restorers who produce the objets d'art coveted all over the world.

In the two thousand years of Tuscan history, the population has experienced every form of government, from free commune to republic, from grandduchy to monarchy. In the beginning, the Etruscans cultivated it, the Romans filled it with the cities of Antiquity, the Longobards and Franks dominated it, and the popes (Guelph faction) and the emperors (Ghibelline faction) fought over it. During its golden age—from the 14th to 16th centuries—Florence was ruled by the Medici, whose bankers, merchants, and artists raised it to greatness. During the 18th and 19th centuries, the Austrian dynasty of the Lorraines transformed the Grandduchy of Tuscany into a modern city state. In 1860, the region joined the unified Kingdom of Italy, of which Florence was capital from 1865 to 1870. The upheaval in Italian society which took place after World War II changed Tuscany from a chiefly agricultural region into one of small- and medium-sized industries—over seventy thousand are currently operating—whose origins may be traced back to a thousand-year-long crafts tradition.

A single book would not suffice to recount the great Tuscans and their artistic and intellectual achievements: Dante and Boccaccio invented modern Italian; Machiavelli and Guicciardini, modern history; Galileo, modern science. The genius of sculptors such as the Pisano and painters such as Cimabue, Giotto (Florentine school), Duccio, Simone Martini, and the Lorenzetti (Sienese school) paved the way for the celebrated Renaissance masters who need no introduction: Masaccio, Brunelleschi, Piero della Francesca, Donatello, Botticelli, Fra Angelico, Leonardo, and Michelangelo—all of whom we shall meet on the following pages.

Many cuisines, one prize

Poised between Northern Italian cuisine based on rice, butter, and lemon and Southern Italian cuisine based on pasta and olive oil, Tuscan cuisine is based on a wide variety of breads, olive oils, and wines. Possibly of Etruscan origin, it consists of simple country dishes without elaborate sauces and dressings. Tuscany is renowned for the quality of its fruit and vegetables (still called "erbe"), especially legumes such as beans, chickpeas, and the newly rediscovered farro. Many popular dishes can be found throughout the region—but be careful because they can have different names in different places. Tuscans have always been convivial eaters and drinkers, so it is not surprising that the first Corporazione degli Osti (Restaurateurs' Guild) was founded in Florence in the Middle Ages. The old canove and buche (taverns) are the forerunners of the ubiquitous pizzicherie (grocery stores filled with delicious gourmet treats) and trattorie (informal restaurants where the food is often better and less expensive than in the ristoranti).

The influence of Tuscan cuisine has been growing ever since 1533, when Caterina de' Medici moved to Paris to marry Henry II, King of France, accompanied by her Tuscan chefs. According to a recent count, four thousand chefs originally from Al-topascio, near Lucca, practice their art in cities all over the world.

Each area of Tuscany vaunts its own specialties: In Pisa, Leghorn, and all along the coast, the specialties are mostly seafood dishes such as cacciucco fish stew and cieche eels (literally, "blind ones," as the newborn eels are called). Maremma is where wild boars are hunted and cooked in agrodolce (sweet and sour) sauce. The plains of Lucca and Garfagnana are renowned for the unrivaled quality of the locally grown beans, asparagus, spinach, fennel, artichokes. Siena is famous for its soft pici pasta and hard, chewy desserts. The specialties of Florence include the country-style first courses ribollita (bread soup), pappa al pomodoro (tomato soup), and panzanella (bread salad), as well as trippa alla fiorentina (cow stomachs in tomato sauce), pollo all'arrabbiata (spicy chicken), and bistecca alla fiorentina (Florentine-style steak, which was originally brought to Florence by the British, but made famous by the Florentines).

Tuscan wines, several of which are world famous, deserve a space of their own. So, we have dedicated three wine reports to them, which you can consult at the end of this chapter.

THE RENAISSANCE REPAST REPORT

A banquet at the Medici Court

In the early 1600s, in the course of a historic day-long banquet held by the Medici in Palazzo Vecchio, twenty-four cold dishes were served, followed by numerous hot dishes and desserts.

The banquet as a theatrical spectacle

The Renaissance banquets were among the great events of court life. Not just long dinner parties, they were elaborate theatrical spectacles, with the guests, or players, seated according to strict rules, and hordes of servants, or supporting players, performing their duties according to carefully planned scripts. In addition to being served between twenty and thirty elaborate courses, the guests were treated to surprises such as little birds concealed in their napkins that would fly into the air when the napkins were unfolded or mirrors concealed beneath the tablecloth so that at the end of the meal the guests found themselves staring into their own reflections. The great architect and designer Bernardo Buontalenti served as the **"Sovrintendente della Festa"** (i.e., the person in charge of table settings, food and drink, and entertainment) at many celebrated banquets.

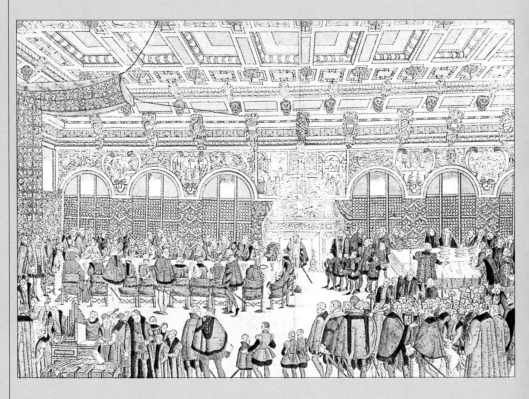

Scalchi, trincianti, and table manners

In Renaissance times, the man in charge of the banquet table, often of noble rank, was called the *"Scalco."* He choreographed the servants as they served course after course and supervised the *Trinciante,* whose job it was to artistically carve the meat with a two-pronged fork and a set of knives. Other nobles were in charge of setting the tables.

A team of *Coppieri* poured the wines and brought the guests the little water basins known as *rinfrescatoi* (refreshers) so they could rinse their hands. Guests of espe-

According to legend, French cuisine originated from the Florentine tradition carried to France by Caterina de' Medici (b. 1517), the daughter of Lorenzo, Duke of Urbino, when she married King Henry II. (She is also said to have introduced forks, an implement hitherto unknown to the French.)

Whether the story is true or not, it is undeniable that, starting from the time of Lorenzo the Magnificent in the second half of the 15th century, banquets were highly elaborate events. The Medici continued the tradition of holding sumptuous banquets until the end of the 17th century (when Cosimo III de' Medici thrilled his guests with delicious sherbet desserts).

In a Medici banquet held in Palazzo Vecchio, the assortment of twenty-four cold dishes included peacock, capon pie, white sugar cakes, lamprey stuffed with cream, cow's tongue, chicken with pears, and pigeon. There were also cakes, pies, truffle pies, peaches in wine, pears, as well as candied pears, grapes, and apples.

Today, nobody would ever think of eating so much. But in those days banquets were above all spectacles.

Above: detail of Supper at Emmaus
by Pontormo (left).
Caterina de' Medici *in a portrait by François Clouet* (right).
Below: drawing *showing utensils used in Renaissance banquets* .
Above right*: a Renaissance court banquet.*

A fascinating aspect of history regards food: how it was prepared, the utensils used in cooking and serving, and the various kinds of table settings. The first source of information is painting. In Florentine works of the 14th-16th centuries, there are numerous depictions of tables in religious scenes such as the Last Supper, the Banquet of Herod, Christ in the House of the Pharisee, and the lives of the saints. The second source, archeology, provides information regarding the daily life of the common people. Recent excavations in Florence of wells and landfills have brought to light jars, plates, and utensils in ceramic, glass, and metal. (Objects in perishable materials such as wood and bone have evidently not come down to us.) The third source is documentary evidence, i.e., written accounts of court life and ledgers listing the various expenses for kitchen items and food.

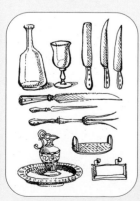

cially high rank had not one, but two *Coppieri* to attend to their needs.
In the Middle Ages, there were no forks or plates. Instead, people grabbed what they wanted from a round wooden cutting-board known as the *"tagliere"* set in the center of the table and used their hands to get food to their mouths. They drank out of metal cups. It is said that glasses became popular only when suspicious people wanted to see the color of the liquid they were about to drink to avoid being poisoned.

Seven centuries and then revolution

*A trip through the Tuscan countryside is an unforgettable experience
of discovery an immense open-air museum*

The 15th century painting of a Tuscan landscape (left) and a contemporary photo of the same scene (right) reveal five centuries of splendid timelessness. The urbanization that revolutionized the countryside occurred after World War II. In the last fifty years, farmers have plummeted from 40 percent to 4.7 percent of the total population.

At the same time, the depopulation of the rural areas has been accompanied by a steady increase in the mechanization of grape and olive cultivation so that Tuscany ranks as one of the country's leading producers of quality wines and olive oils.

The celebrated Tuscan landscape of gently rolling hills and valleys with neat rows of vineyards and cypress trees, dotted with charming farmhouses exudes a feeling of great harmony and peace. Unfortunately, for the reasons we have just listed, its area is being slowly, but steadily, reduced in size.

Tuscany is not only just a region of gently rolling hills and valleys. A large part of its territory is covered with mountains whose forests are rapidly expanding as the population continues to shift to the cities. Over 40 percent of the Italian forests are in Tuscany.

The over one million hectares of forestland are all nature reserves or tourist resorts. The most common forests are beech, fir, pine (prone to forest fires). *Agriturismo* (country vacations) and the restoration of country houses as vacation homes have greatly contributed to the preservation of the Tuscan countryside.

An agriturismo *vacation in Tuscany.*

THE FARM LABOR REPORT

How and where the land provided bread and wine

In addition to being filled with art museums, Tuscany has numerous museums of country life which, in a certain sense, can be considered the archeological museums of Tuscan agriculture They provide the tourist with a fascinating glimpse into how peasants and farmers labored for hundreds of years and illustrate the various crops grown which, interestingly, are once more regaining popularity for genuineness and taste.

❶ PALAZZUOLO SUL SENIO – *MUSEUM OF COUNTRY LIFE*
❷ RUFINA – *MUSEUM OF GRAPES AND WINE*
❸ SAN PELLEGRINO IN ALPE – *MUSEUM OF YESTERYEAR*
❹ MASSA MARITTIMA – *MUSEUM OF COUNTRY LIFE*
❺ BOLGHERI – *MUSEUM OF MENUS*
❻ BUONCONVENTO – *MUSEUM OF BREAD AND HEMP*
❼ SOVICILLE – *STOREHOUSE OF COUNTRY LIFE*

PALAZZUOLO SUL SENIO – *MUSEUM OF COUNTRY LIFE.* The museum has attractive exhibits of farm machinery and equipment, handmade objects, as well as original rooms and furniture from a rural house.

RUFINA – *MUSEUM OF GRAPES AND WINE.* The museum displays more than one thousand objects relating to the cultivation of vineyards and wine-making, including various wine containers and 18th century handblown glass goblets (below).

SAN PELLEGRINO IN ALPE – *MUSEUM OF GRAPES AND WINE* Located by a medieval pilgrims' lodging and a sanctuary in the heart of the Garfagnana region, the museum has

over 3000 objects relating to 19th century rural life, (kitchens, bedrooms, cellars) and crafts and occupations (metal-working, knife-sharpening, and shoe-making tools).

MASSA MARITTIMA – *MUSEUM OF COUNTRY LIFE.* Located in the Fortezza di Monteregio in the heart of the Pisan Maremma region, the museum displays farm equipment and objects relating to rural life in a huge ground-floor room.

BOLGHERI – *MUSEUM OF MENUS.* This museum has an unusual collection of menus from over ten thousand banquets and court dinners held by historic figures such as the Savoy family and Mussolini and by contemporary food experts such as the great French chef Paul Bacause. It also has a well-stocked library (upon).

BUONCONVENTO – *MUSEUM OF BREAD AND HEMP.* Situated along the medieval Via Francigena not far from Siena, this museum documents the production of hemp and its uses and the bread-making process from the wheat plant to the loaf.

SOVICILLE – *STOREHOUSE OF COUNTRY LIFE.* The museum collection includes farm equipment, hand- and animal-driven transportation means, not to mention a superb oil mill.

THE FARMHOUSE REPORT

In these old rooms

Born of the elegant Tuscan rationality of the 18th century, the Tuscan case coloniche *were originally designed as farmhouses. Today, they are becoming increasingly popular with city dwellers, who restore them as vacation homes.*

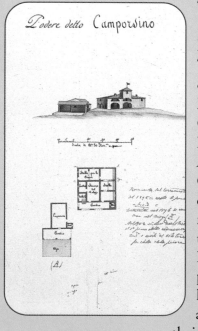

The typical Tuscan *casa colonica* has a loggia and a tower. The original design originated in the late 1700s under Grandduke Pietro Leopoldo at the Accademia dei Georgofili (still today Italy's most renowned agricultural institute). Its aim was to improve the peasants' living conditions and rationalize their labor. Bernardino Della Porta, influenced by the great architect and set-designer Bernardo Buontalenti, was responsible for the design and construction of the prototype, which led to the building of dozens of *case coloniche* in the territories of Siena, Arezzo, and Florence. They are usually perched upon hilltops amid fields planted with cereals, olive groves, vineyards, and rows of cypresses.

Although the case coloniche *are attractive, sturdy, and rationally constructed, many were abandoned during the great exodus from the rural areas to the cities that started in the 1950s. With the reverse exodus, so many have been bought up and restored as elegant vacation homes that the very few still on the market command extremely high prices. Thus, the* case coloniche *have stimulated a return to the country, which has been one of the prime factors in saving Tuscany's architectural heritage.*

More than just a machine

The most striking quality of the Tuscan *casa colonica* is how perfectly it blends in with the landscape, the sun, the elements.

Typically, it is a two-story structure topped by a little tower known as *"colombaia"* (doves' nest).

The facade is broken by a double row of arcading, which on the ground floor creates a loggia and, on the second floor, an arcade.

Like any self-respecting Tuscan farmhouse, the *casa colonica* has a bread oven, a wine-cellar, stalls for the animals, granaries, and a covered dry storage area.

Many of the case coloniche *have been renovated and opened* agriturismo *centers, that offer unforgettable vacations for people who appreciate fresh country air and delicious homegrown, homecooked food.*

Facing page, below: *A plan of an 18th century farmhouse.*
Above: *Farmhouses.*
Lunette: *16th century painting of a Medici villa by Justus Utens.*

Bread—a staple for over 2000 years

Every country has its own breads.
Bread is back—Tuscany's elegant bakeries are like bread boutiques.

There are dozens of kinds of bread—there's bread made with oil, with milk, crackers, sweet rolls—but the classic Tuscan bread is simply water, flour, and salt, leavened with brewer's yeast.

The standard loaf is made with type 0 flour which is mechanically kneaded, divided into portions, and then modeled into the desired shape of loaf. Most Italian breads are baked in electric ovens, but in Tuscany you can still buy *"pane cotto a legna"* (bread baked in a wood-burning oven) which is superior in quality and fragrance.

Every country has its own bread: France has

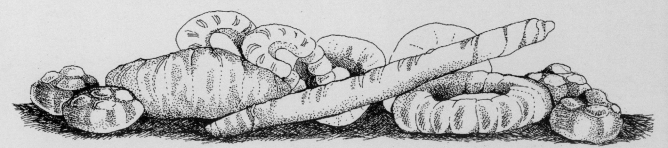

BREAD AND MISERY: centuries of hunger, deceit, and revolution

the crusty *baguette*, Germany and the northern countries have thick, dark breads...In Italy, each region has its own bread.

The outstanding feature of Tuscan bread is that it contains only a tiny bit of salt—so that it won't overpower the taste of the foods it accompanies. The various types of Tuscan breads are illustrated in this report.

Traditionally, Europe and the Mediterranean are bread eaters (whereas Asians are mostly rice eaters). In Antiquity, European bread was unleavened. The Romans used to eat flat rolls until, as the naturalist Pliny recounts, yeast was discovered.

The bakers' guilds were founded during the time of the communes in the Middle Ages. The modern concept of bakery goods originated in the 16th century, when grapes, almonds, spices, and honey were added to various kinds of dough.

In Tuscany as in Italy and in many parts of Europe, bread was traditionally the staple of the common people, especially the peasants—actually, it was virtually all they had to eat from the Middle Ages to the 18th century.

Bread was one of the ruling class's chief concerns: whether to raise or lower its price, how much it could or should be taxed, and how to control the distribution of wheat (grown only in Apulia and Sicily) to combat the recurrent famines which broke out.

When the poor could not afford bread made of wheat—which was often—they ate substitutes: If they lived in the mountains, they ate bread made of chestnut flour and, after the discovery of America, they made bread out of corn.

During periods of famine, the peasants were often driven by hunger to eat the wheat reserved for seeds which added to their immediate misery and their long-

THE BREAD REPORT

term dependence on their landlords. *In Tuscany, the peasants and laborers would often turn to what was termed "pane ignobile" (ignoble bread), a bread made of dough "spiked" with hallucinogenic plants or herbs such as poppy seeds, that would assuage their hunger and fatigue and provide them with the artificial energy to continue their labor.*

In short, bread—be it "the bread of princes" or "bread fit for dogs"— is Europe's oldest and most popular food. For centuries, whenever it was scarce, there was an uprising, or even a revolution, of the hungry masses to whom it was indispensable for life.

"Give us our daily bread"

"Give us our daily bread" recites the Lord's Prayer, the most important of the Christian prayers, where bread is the food of life. The New Testament recounts how Christ broke bread and drank wine at the Last Supper, entrusting his continuing presence among men to bread and wine.

In the Jewish tradition, unleavened bread is eaten during Passover. In keeping with this practice, the Christian Eucharist is made of unleavened bread. Moreover, after the Second Vatican Council, some of the Oriental Christian churches have also incorporated the use of bread into their rites.

Bread-baking is an art in Tuscany, especially when it's done in a wood-burning oven.
Above: Last Supper *by Domenico Ghirlandaio, Ognissanti, Florence.*

The hundred uses of bread

Owing to its simplicity and country origin, the Tuscan cuisine features a large number of special dishes in which bread is the main ingredient. Among these are three of the most famous Florentine specialties, ribollita *(bread and vegetable soup),* pappa al pomodoro *(bread and tomato soup), and* panzanella *(bread and vegetable salad). (These are discussed in detail in the chapter on Florence.) Other Tuscan bread specialties are* cofaccino *(flat bread) in the Pistoia mountains, bread soups such as* pagnone *(stale bread soup),* panata *(dry or toasted bread soup) in the Casentino region, and* zuppa del Seghetti *(bread and wine soup) and* zuppa matta *(salad of stale bread with spring onions and other vegetables) in the regions of Pisa, Leghorn, and Lucca.*

THE TUSCAN TABLE
Antipasto and first courses

TUSCAN GARLIC BREAD (FETTUNTA)

Fettunta, or *bruschetta*, is a great snack or appetizer.
Ingredients: country-style bread, cut in thick slices; peeled

garlic; olive oil; salt and pepper.

Toast bread slices, preferably over a wood-burning fire. Rub garlic on hot slices and add salt, pepper, and abundant olive oil. Serve hot.

TUSCAN OPEN CHOPPED LIVER SANDWICHES (CROSTINI DI FEGATINI)

This is one of the many recipes for Tuscan chopped liver.
Ingredients: 200 grams of chicken livers, washed and dried; 1 onion, minced; 4 tablespoons of olive oil; *vinsanto*; 1 tablespoon of butter; capers; anchovies; broth; country-style bread, cut in thick slices.

Serves four
Sauté onion in four tablespoons of olive oil. Add chicken livers and a drop of vinsanto and cook for 15 minutes. Remove the chicken livers, cut into small pieces, and return to pan. Add butter, capers, and anchovies and cook for 15 minutes. Smooth spread on sandwich slices and serve.

VEGETABLE BREAD SOUP (RIBOLLITA)

Ribollita, perhaps Tuscany's best-known specialty, owes its name (reboiled) to its origin as a vegetable soup that is boiled again the day after it is first made. Under no circumstances should it be made with canned beans!
Ingredients: 300 grams of dry *cannellini* beans; 6 tablespoons of olive oil; 1 onion, minced; 1 clove of garlic; 1 stalk celery, minced; 1 carrot, sliced; tomatoes, diced; beet greens; cabbage; black cabbage; country-style bread, sliced; salt and pepper.

Serves four
Cook cannellini *beans, drain, and mash, setting aside a few whole beans. Sauté onion, garlic, celery, and carrot. Add tomatoes, beet greens, cabbage, black cabbage, and salt and pepper. Add beans, and cook for one hour, adding the whole beans. Pour over slices of bread placed in a soup bowl. Let stand for half hour. Serve with a sprinkle of olive oil.*

PAPPARDELLE NOODLES WITH HARE SAUCE (PAPPARDELLE SULLA LEPRE)

Pappardelle are homemade egg noodles, three-four centimeters in width and less than one millimeter thick.
Ingredients: *pappardelle*; forepart (including shoulder), liver, blood of a hare; cut into bite-size bits; 1 onion, minced; 1 carrot, minced; 1 stalk celery, minced; bacon; grated parmesan cheese; wine; sliced truffles (optional); olive oil; salt and pepper.

Sauté onion, carrot, and celery, with bacon in olive oil. Add hare bits and cook until liquid thickens. Add wine and hare's blood. Cook until done. Debone hare and add liver. Flavor with salt and pepper to taste. Pour hare sauce on pappardelle *cooked al dente. Add grated cheese and truffles.*

TOMATO BREAD SOUP (PAPPA AL POMODORO)

This is the classic recipe for *pappa al pomodoro*, which is just as delicious—if not more so—reheated the day after. A leek may be substituted for the clove of garlic.
Ingredients: 300 grams country-style bread baked in a wood-burning oven, sliced; 1 clove of garlic; 1 chili pepper; basil; 1.5 kg of ripe tomatoes (fresh or canned); broth; salt and pepper.

Sauté garlic and chili pepper and add basil and tomatoes. When mixture boils, add broth and bread. Cook for a few minutes. Let stand for at least one hour and serve with olive oil and a dash of pepper.

THE QUALITY CERTIFICATION REPORT

For healthy unadulterated food and drink

Tuscan products certified by the European Union

All the foods on this page have been awarded Italian or European Union certification

There are four kinds of quality certification:

Doc – *Denominazione di origine controllata* (Italian certification)

Docg – *Denominazione di origine controllata e garantita* (Italian certification)

Dop – *Denominazione di origine protetta* (EU certification)

Igp – *Indicazione geografica protetta* (EU certification).

Tuscan wines: Thirty-six Tuscan wines have Doc certification and three (Chianti, Brunello di Montalcino, and Carmignano) have Docg certification.

Tuscan *pecorino*: Tuscan *pecorino* cheese has Dop certification. A consortium of producers monitors product quality to ensure that it is made of pure sheep's milk from sheep that have grazed in grass pasturelands.

Tuscan ham: Tuscan ham has Dop certification. A consortium of producers ensures that the animals are slaughtered at not less than nine months old and that they weigh between 144-176 kilo-grams. Frozen meat is not allowed. No more than 100,000 hams a year are produced.

Mugello chestnuts: Chestnuts from the Mugello have Igp certification. No chemical fertilizers may be used and the edible part must be fine-grained and very sweet.

Garfagnana *farro*: *Farro* from the Garfagnana has Igp certification. *Farro*, one of the oldest known cereals, was popular with the Romans in Antiquity. It is still hulled on the mills' old stone grinders.

Tuscan olive oil. Tuscan olive oil has quality certification regarding both the olives and the oil. (See "The Olive Oil Report.")

Food Festival Calendar

FLORENCE

December	Barberino Val D'Elsa	*Fettunta* Festival
September	Impruneta	Grape Festival
October	Marradi	Chestnut Festival
June	San Godenzo	*Pecorino* Cheese Festival

PRATO

August	Carmignano	Fig Festival

PISTOIA

August	Lamporecchio	*Brigidino* Festival
March-August	Marliana	Pancake Festival
August	Ponte Buggianese	Ice cream Festival

LUCCA

July	Molazzana	Pie Festival
August	Porcari	Toad Festival

In addition to the artistic beauties we have admired in our travels about Tuscany, there are other wonderful places to visit, festas to enjoy, and country food to savor. An old Tuscan fair is illustrated in the painting below.

LEGHORN

June-July	Collesalvetti	Spaghetti Festival
April	Piombino	Artichoke Festival

PISA

June-July	Buti	Toad Festival
May	Lari	Ham and Bean Festival
October	San Miniato	Mushroom and Truffles Festival
June	Vecchiano	Pizza Festival

GROSSETO

July	Capalbio	Fish Festival
May	Manciano	Snail Festival
August	Montieri	Steak Festival
July	Orbetello	Eel Festival

AREZZO

August	Bibbiena	Watermelon Festival
October	Caprese Michelangelo	Country Fair
May	Castiglion Fiorentino	Boar Festival
March	Cavriglia	Snail Festival
July	Montemignaio	Trout Festival
August	Poppi	Toad Festival

SIENA

August	Castellina in Chianti	Watermelon Festival

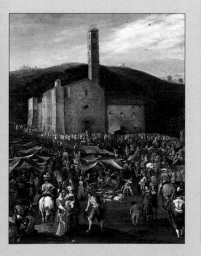

With prayer and elisir

Tuscany's historical monasteries, abbeys, and sanctuaries are both tourist attractions and pilgrimage sites. You'll be able to see fascinating places and taste the monks' delicious spices, liquors, and food.

1 Monastery of San Miniato al Monte

2 Chartreuse of Florence

3 Monastery-Sanctuary of Monte Senario

4 Abbey of Santa Maria di Rosano

5 Monastery of Santa Maria, Istituto Cristo Re

6 Abbey of Vallombrosa

7 Sanctuary of La Verna

8 Monastery and Hermitage of Camaldoli

9 Abbey of Monte Oliveto Maggiore

10 Chartreuse of Calci (Pisa)

11 Abbey of Montenero

12 Chartreuse of Farneta

*Other noteworthy religious monuments include the abbey of **Santissimo Salvatore**, the abbey of **San Salvatore** near Monte Amiata; the monastery of **San Vivaldo** between Certaldo and Volterra, the picturesque abbey of **San Galgano** (below) between Siena and Grosseto, and the abbey of **Sant'Antimo** near Montalcino (Siena).*

Monastic life: a thousand-year treasure

The word "monastery" comes from the Greek expression for "place where people live alone." Monastic life originated in the East, and spread throughout Christian Europe after St. Benedict of Norcia dictated his famous Rule.

The Benedictine monks are skilled workers and experts in copying (and today in restoring) old manuscripts. Reformed Benedictines include the Clunian, Vallombrosan, Camaldolesan, and Cistercian orders. The Trappists are especially rigorous and ascetic. Many monasteries and abbeys are under the supervision of the Franciscans, Dominicans, Agostinians, Olivetans, and Carmelites.

Florence and environs

San Miniato al Monte. The church of San Miniato al Monte, with its splendid two-color facade, rises above Piazzale Michelangelo. Built in the 11th century, it has been an Olivetan

monastery since 1373. Inside are masterpieces such as the *Cappella del Crocifisso* designed by **Michelozzo** in 1448, the *tomb of the Cardinal of Portugal* by **Antonio Rossellino**, and the Chiostro Maggiore.

An excellent assortment of liquors, including Sambuca Goccia Amara, Elisir di Caffè, and Liquore Flora flavored with herbs, honey, and olive oil, produced by the Abbey of Monte Oliveto Maggiore, are on sale.

Monastery-Sanctuary of Monte Senario. Not far from Pratolino is the 14th century monastery-sanctuary of Monte Senario situated in a cypress wood. It is adorned with fine panel paintings and sculptures.

For over a century, the Servi di Maria monks have been producing and selling renowned liquors such as tangy, balsamic Gemma d'Abete, Elisir di China, Alchermes (sweet), and Amaro Borghini (bitter).

Abbey of Santa Maria di Rosano. Only fifteen kilometers from Florence at Pontassieve, the Abbey of Santa Maria di Rosano, founded in 780 by the Benedictine cloistered nuns, has a Romanesque church and a *cloister* designed by **Michelozzo**.

The nuns produce and sell Chianti wines, herb liquors, honey, jams, pottery, and fine embroideries.

Monastery of Santa Maria – Istituto di Cristo Re Sommo Sacerdote. *The monastery is renowned for Gregorian chants it puts on and the genuine products such as Chianti Putto wines, dessert wines, and olive oil sold in the outlet.*

The Chartreuse of Florence

Perched on the hill overlooking Galluzzo, the Chartreuse of Florence was founded by Niccolò Acciaioli in 1341 as a Certosan monastery. It has been a Cistercian monastery for the last fifty years. Among its art treasures are *frescoes* by *Pontormo* and paintings by *Fra Angelico* and Sebastiano Ricci. It has fine 16th century choir stalls and three remarkable cloisters.

The monks sell exquisite honey and jams, violet and lily-of-the-valley lavender, and liquors (Gran Certosa, Elisir di San Bernardo, Rosolio al Mandarino, and Gocce Imperiali).

The apothecaries

The monastery apothecaries are the forerunners of modern-day pharmacies. From their inception, all the monasteries were hospitals and cultivated herbal gardens. As the monks became experts in the art of healing with the medicinal plants they

themselves distilled, they opened their apothecaries to all of the surrounding territory. Today, the apothecaries produce and sell rare distilled herbs, liquors, and perfumes. They are remarkable places, with old wooden cabinets, ceramic jars, and glass instruments. One of the oldest is the internationally renowned *Officina Profumo Farmaceutica di Santa Maria Novella* in Florence.

Tuscany's abbeys and monasteries

Abbey of Vallombrosa. In a picturesque, heavily forested setting near Reggello rises the abbey of Vallombrosa, which was founded by St. Giovanni Gualberto in 1028 and remodeled in 1470. Of note are the organ, the dining hall, the cloister, and the glazed *terracottas* by **Luca Della Robbia**.

The monks sell trout (from their own fish-farm) and liquors: Amaro Ottanta (herb mixture), Vallombrosa dry gin (made of juniper), and Liquore Tonico Digestivo (a digestive).

Spirits

The popular liquors such as tonics, digestives, and corroborants produced in the convents and monasteries are based on old recipes, many of which have been secret for centuries.

Monastery-Sanctuary of La Verna. Here, 1283 meters above sea level in the heart of the Casentino, St. Francis received the stigmata. The monastery-sanctuary of La Verna which grew up on the site of the miracle is adorned with glazed *terracottas* by the **Della Robbia** family and numerous picturesque cloisters.

Its liquors (Amaro della Verna, Cordiale Amabile della Verna, and Laverna gin) are renowned. It hosts a popular Organ Festival in July and August.

Monastery and Hermitage of Camaldoli

The monastery and hermitage of Camaldoli are actually three kilometers apart in a sacred forest of firs and beeches over one thousand meters above sea level. The monastery, founded in 980, was donated to St. Romualdo, who inaugurated the first five cells of the hermitage in 1012. Today, there are twenty cells belonging to the *Congregazione Camaldolese*. In the monastery, one of the most celebrated sites of monastic life, are *paintings* by **Lorenzo Lippi** and **Giorgio Vasari** and a noteworthy dining hall.

The pharmacy, whose products are stocked in old jars and mortars, has been operating since 1513. In addition to liquors (Elisir dell'Eremita and Lacrima d'Abeto), the monks sell infusions, honey, chocolate, liquor candies, chestnuts, black currants, and a well-known line of cosmetics.

Abbey of Monte Oliveto Maggiore

The great complex constituting the abbey of Monte Oliveto Maggiore rises in the Sienese countryside near Asciano. Today, the headquarters of the Olivetan Benedictine order, it was founded in 1319 by St. Bernardo Tolomei. It has always been a center of art and culture. Among the noteworthy sights are masterpieces by *Signorelli* and *Sodoma*, the library containing a precious collection of illuminated manuscripts, and the Istituto di Patologia del Libro, which specializes in restoring books.

The monks sell excellent liquors (Liquore Flora, Sambuca Goccia Amara, and Coffee Elisir di Caffè), as well as honey and olive oil.

Abbey-Sanctuary of Montenero. Rising on a hill near Leghorn and dedicated to the Madonna delle Grazie, the abbey-sanctuary of Montenero is the oldest in Tuscany. According to legend, the painting of the Virgin was carried here by angels. According to art history, it is a 14th century panel painting. Today run by the Vallombrosan monks, it is famous for its *ex-voto* images (naïf paintings) donated to the Virgin for her miraculous interventions.

The monks sell liquor (Liquore Giallo and Liquore Verde), honey, and candies in the old pharmacy.

Chartreuse of Farneta. The splendid 14th century chartreuse of Farneta is located near Lucca. Its major treasure is the *Reliquary of the Holy Cross*, a masterpiece of Byzantine art.

The Capuchin Franciscan monks are famous for the liquors (Gran Liquore Certosa Verde with fifteen kinds of herbs and citrus rinds, Gran Liquore Certosa Giallo, Elisir di Caffè, Amaretto, Rum, Alchermes, China, Amaro Certosino, and lastly, the Elisir della Salute, which is a mixture of herbs, wine, and resins).

You can admire masterpieces such as this Annunciation by Andrea Della Robbia, in the peace and quiet of La Verna.

Chartreuse of Calci (Pisa). Majestically rising in a verdant setting of cypress and olive trees, the chartreuse of Calci was founded in 1366 and remodeled several times in the course of the centuries. It has a picturesque cloister. Of note are the huge dining hall, the monks' cemetery, the church, and the **Museo Storico Artistico**, a natural history museum with a collection of cetaceans, birds, and minerals.

THE COFFEE REPORT

From Islamic brew to *espresso*

Coffee originated in the East in the 14th century when the Arabs discovered how to roast coffee beans and "invented" the dark-colored liquid known as "Islamic brew." The first coffeehouses were opened in Constantinopolis in 1554. Coffee reached Italy via Turkish merchant ships. In 1720, during the Enlightenment, when the Caffè alla Venezia Trionfante was inaugurated in Venice, coffee represented intellectual vigor and a modern outlook—as opposed to chocolate, which was the old-fashioned drink of the aristocratic classes. Coffeehouses soon became popular all over Italy, including Tuscany. Some of them are still operating today.

A tour of the most celebrated Tuscan coffeehouses

Some coffeehouses are over a century old. They were the sites of patriotic encounters and artistic debates between those who spent their time and those with time to spend.

IN FLORENCE

Caffè Rivoire in Piazza della Signoria in front of Palazzo Vecchio has been renowned for its hot chocolate since 1872. **Caffè Giacosa** has been a landmark on one of Florence's most famous shopping streets, Via Tornabuoni, for almost a century. There are several renowned coffeehouses in Piazza della Repubblica: **Giubbe Rosse** (literally, red jackets, from the color of the waiters' uniforms), patronized by, among others, Andrè Gide, Lenin, and Montale, was where a good part of 20th Italian literature was born (and where cultural events are still held today). **Caffè Paszkowski**, a meeting place for the Florentine social and cultural elite since the end of World War II, holds live concerts in summer. **Caffè Gilli**, renowned for its fine pastry, has been lovingly restored to its original Art Nouveau splendor.

IN PISTOIA

Caffè Valiani, located in a building which was originally a 14th century oratory in the historic center of Pistoia, has been in business for over 150 years. Inside, its walls

There are two different ways of making coffee. The first is to pour coarsely ground coffee over boiling water to produce an infusion. A variant of this method is Turkish coffee.

The second is the Italian method of percolating finely ground coffee through a stream of boiling water. The coffee can be made in a Neapolitan coffeepot, a Moka

are covered with original paintings, historic documents, and old photos. It serves excellent coffee.

IN MONTECATINI
One of the most elegant spots in the elegant spa of Montecatini, **Caffè Gambrinus** has preserved its original appearance of a turn-of-the-century open-air caffè-concerto.

IN LUCCA
Caffè Caselli-Di Simo, located on one Italy's loveliest streets, Via Fillungo, looks like an old London club with its fancy mirrors, elegant furnishings, and lovely coffee cups; it is a popular meeting place for artists and writers. Inaugurated in 19839, **Caffè delle Mura** (coffeehouse of the walls) is located, as its name suggests, along the city walls.

IN PISA
The history of the city and university of Pisa is closely linked to the celebrated **Caffè dell'Ussero**. Popular with Pisa University students from the time of its opening at the end of the 18th century, it has served the likes of Alfieri, Byron, Leopardi, and Carducci.

IN SIENA
There are several **Caffè Nannini** in Siena, all run by the Nannini Company, the producer of Siena's famous panforte e di ricciarelli cakes, and, not surprisingly, famous for their pastry.

Caffè Giubbe Rosse, *Florence* (above left); Caffè Valiani, *Pistoia* (above right),
and Caffè Caseli-DeSimo, *Lucca* (above).
The photos of coffeepots and cups are taken from Dal Caffè all'Espresso, *by Francesco and Riccardo Illy, the celebrated coffee-producers.*

coffeepot, or an *espresso* machine. A striking *espresso* machine designed by Giugiaro appears in the photo on the left.

Since *espresso* is an emulsion and a suspension at the same time, it has aroma and texture as well as taste. *Espresso* should be served in a warm cup thick enough to absorb part of the heat from the coffee.

Tea or coffee? Two different worlds

Once upon a time, everyone's favorite drink was chocolate. Today, the most popular drinks are tea and coffee. The Earth's population is divided into two groups: the coffee drinkers and the tea drinkers. Coffee, which originated in the East, has become the most popular drink in the West. Since the 18th century, it has been a symbol of intellectual lucidity, a bit exotic and even erotic—its strong flavor and black color do recall hell. It did not become popular immediately. The renowned physician-poet Francesco Redi was a staunch critic of coffee for many years at the 17th century court of Grandduke Cosimo de' Medici—until he, too, converted to the "Islamic brew."

The superbly appointed *Teatro della Pergola* (right) is one of the oldest—having been built in the 17th century—and best known theaters in Italy. Since 1932, the *Teatro Comunale* (far right) has hosted the *Maggio Musicale Fiorentino*, the renowned international festival of opera and symphonic music.

The Biennale Antiques Exhibition

Florence has been an antiques center for centuries. By "antiques," the Florentines mean everything from hand-crafted objects and furniture to the adornments of portals, windows, and gardens of palaces.

Since 1959, it has hosted the prestigious *Biennale Internazionale dell'Antiquariato*, which draws collectors and dealers from all over the world. When the Biennale is not in session, you can admire the rarities in the antiques shops lining Via Maggio and Via dei Fossi and in and around the picturesque **Flea Market** in Piazza dei Ciompi.

FLORENCE

One of the world's great art cities, it has a thousand charms

Wood-carving (above) and book-binding (below) are still common occupations in many neighborhoods of the historic center. Florentine artisans produce picture frames, leather goods, and embroideries, as well as objects in bronze, wrought iron, wood, precious stones, and marble—some of which are veritable *objets d'art*.

Picturesque outdoor markets abound. The *Mercato della Paglia* (Straw Market; upper left) located under a 16th century arcade, the *Loggia del Mercato Nuovo* (New Market), specializes in leather goods and embroidery. On the south side is the *Fontana del Porcellino*, the bronze boar fountain designed by Pietro Tacca in 1612. Florence's *Flea Market*, open daily in centrally located Piazza dei Ciompi, offers both antiques and bric-a-brac.

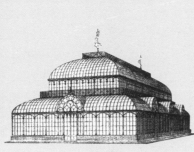

Florence is full of gardens, many of which are not visible from the street. Noteworthy are the 16th century *Orto Botanico* (Botanical Garden) and the *Giardino dell'Orticoltura* (Horticulture Garden). The striking Art Nouveau *Tepidario* (left) in the Giardino dell'Orticoltura was built of cast-iron and glass in 1880 and is now being restored. The internationally renowned *Giardino dell'Iris* (Iris Garden, far left), adjoining Piazzale Michelangelo, vaunts 2500 varieties of the flower which for centuries has symbolized Florence.

Eight centuries of master craftsmen

The superb quality Florentine craftsmanship is appreciated throughout the world. Master craftsmen have been producing *objets d'art* made of leather, textiles, wood, bronze, gold, precious stones, and ceramics for centuries—sometimes in tiny workshops that have been used for the same purpose since the Middle Ages.

More recently, designers such as **Gucci**, **Ferragamo**, and **Pucci** have become leaders of the fashion industry.

Since 1931, Florence has hosted the **Mostra Mercato Internazionale dell'Artigianato**, which has become one of Italy's premiere international arts-and-crafts exhibitions.

streets, markets, shops, theaters, parks, avenues

Florence has some remarkable streets: *Via Tornabuoni* (upper right), once the bed of the Mugnone River and now lined with palatial buildings, is one of the most fashionable shopping streets in Italy. *Via Maggio* (lower right), on the other side of the river, is also lined with Renaissance palaces where today some of Florence's most prominent antiques shops are located.

Florence's picturesque *vinai* (minuscule wine bars, above), *osterie* (taverns), and *trippai* (tripe stalls) descend from the medieval *"canove"* (wine shops) and the *Corporazioni degli Osti*. The *trippai* (top) dispense sandwiches packed with steaming cow interiors.

The Festival of the Explosion of the Cart

A centuries-long tradition, the festival of the explosion of the cart takes place on the day before Easter. During the Mass, the Archbishop lights a mechanical dove, which is propelled along a metal wire attached to the main altar on one end and to a wooden cart on the other. When the dove reaches the cart in the middle of the square amid the assembled crowd, fireworks and sparklers explode. The success (or lack of it) of the dove's mechanical "flight" has traditionally been a premonitory sign of how the season's crops will turn out. According to legend, the flints used to set off the dove's flight were brought to Florence from the Holy Sepulcher by Crusader Pazzino de' Pazzi. Hence, the Pazzi family was charged with the maintenance of the cart until the 19th century, when the responsibility passed to the city government. The cart used today—which the Florentines call *"Il Brindellone"* (the oversize banner)—was built in 1622.

Right: *the* Baptistery, *possibly Florence's oldest monument.* Far right: Byzantine mosaics *in the* Baptistery *dome.* Above: aerial view of *the* Baptistery, Duomo, *and Giotto's* Belltower.

The amazing dome over the Duomo, the Baptistery, and Giotto's Belltower

Brunelleschi's Dome among the architectural masterpieces in Piazza del Duomo

On Piazza del Duomo stand some of the world's most celebrated masterpieces of religious art and architecture. The oldest is the **Baptistery**, which Dante called his "beautiful St. John." The most elegant is **Giotto's Belltower**, which resembles a gigantic inlaid jewel. The most majestic is the **Duomo** (cathedral of Santa Maria del Fiore) crowned by **Brunelleschi's dome**, which is an engineering feat just as much as a masterpiece of art. The least known is the **Museo dell'Opera del Duomo** (Cathedral Museum), despite its plethora of masterpieces, including **Michelangelo's** *Pietà*.

The octagonal **Baptistery**, begun in the 6th century and rebuilt in the 11th century, has a striking green and white striped marble facing, typical of the Tuscan Romanesque style. At each of the three entrances is a famous bronze portal: The *south door*, by **Andrea Pisano**, has twenty-eight scenes from the life of St. John the Baptist.

The *north* and *east doors* were designed by **Lorenzo Ghiberti**. The north doors have twenty-eight scenes from the life of Christ. The east doors, known as the *"Doors to Paradise"* and universally acclaimed as Ghiberti's masterpiece, have ten Old Testament scenes in a transition style

the Baptistery contains many remarkable works of art, not least of which is the inlaid marble floor.

The *baptismal font* is a 14th century Pisan school sculpture. On the wall is the *tomb of Pope John XXIII* carved by **Donatello** and **Michelozzo**. The Byzantine mosaics with scenes of the *Last Judgment* in the dome have been attributed to 13th and 14th century Venetian and Florentine master craftsmen, who followed preparatory drawings by **Cimabue** and **Coppo di Marcovaldo**.

On the south side of the square is the **Loggia del Bigallo**, an elegant Gothic construction

And, for dinner, a gigantic bistecca alla fiorentina

According to Florence's *Accademia della Bistecca* (Steak Academy), the perfect Florentine steak must be 3-4.5 centimeters thick, broiled over hot coals (as opposed to a gas fire) until it is brown on the outside and pink (never red) on the inside, and

salted only after cooking. The best meat comes from Valdichiana cows. Actually, having been introduced by English residents in the 18th century, *bistecca alla fiorentina* did not really originate in Florence. However, as a masterpiece of understatement and simplicity—two wholly Florentine culinary characteristics—it may be viewed as the counterbalance to the Florentines' traditional overwhelming preference for vegetables, cereals, and legumes doused in Tuscan olive oil.

between Gothic and Renaissance. Funded by the Merchants' Guild, they took Ghiberti over two decades to sculpt. The interior of

designed in the mid-1300s by Alberto Arnoldi. Inside the *tabernacles* are statues of St. Peter, the Virgin and Child, and St. Lucy.

Doors of Paradise by Lorenzo Ghiberti, **Baptistery,** *Florence.*

Piazza del Duomo has been the religious center of Florence since the 4th century, when a church dedicated to St. Reparata was built next to the Baptistery. In 1128, the church of Santa Reparata was elevated to cathedral status, but it was soon physically and spiritually inadequate for the growing needs of the populace. In 1289, the **Comune** decided to build a new cathedral—a cathedral that would be the biggest, the most magnificent, and the most impressive in Tuscany. (Today, it ranks as the second largest church in the world, after St. Peter's in Rome.) Arnolfo di Cambio was commissioned to design the building and renovate the surrounding area. His design included a dome and a two-color facade to match the Baptistery facing. Arnolfo died in 1302: The dome was built

The 19th century facade of the Duomo. Right: interior of the Duomo. Above: the stupendous dome designed and built by Filippo Brunelleschi. Facing page: Giotto's Belltower.

by Filippo Brunelleschi between 1420 and 1436 and the facade was built in the 19th century by De Fabris.

The **Duomo** was built over the church of Santa Reparata, whose underground crypt came to light after the 1966 flood. Visitors can descend from the Duomo to the crypt, which contains, among fascinating remains of the old church, the tomb of Filippo Brunelleschi.

The immense interior is plain, but majestic. Some of the major events in Florentine history have taken place here. Probably the most famous was the 1478 Pazzi Conspiracy, during which the Pazzi, rivals of the Medici, attacked Lorenzo the Magnificent and his brother, Giuliano during a service. Fra Savonarola, the 15th century reformer friar burned as a heretic, would read his sermons from the Duomo pulpit. The inner facade has a 15th century *clock* with heads of prophets painted by **Paolo Uccello**. On the left aisle wall are two celebrated 15th century frescoes: The *equestrian monument to John Hawkwood* by **Paolo Uccello** and the *equestrian monument to Niccolò da Tolentino* by **Andrea del Castagno**. The octagonal carved *choir* screen enclosing the main altar is by **Baccio Bandinelli**; the wood *crucifix* above it, by **Benedetto da Maiano**. The inside of the dome is wholly covered with a huge fresco of the *Last Judgment* by **Giorgio Vasari** and **Federico Zuccari**, which has recently been restored.

On the outside, the dome is faced in red Impruneta brick with white marble ribbing and topped by a great golden globe (1436). It makes a truly awesome sight. In building it, Brunelleschi did not use a full-scale wooden model, as would have been the normal procedure of his contemporaries. Instead, he devised a novel solution, that of using a mobile scaffolding to work on a section at a time. The scaffolding, comprising an inner

And, for lunch, a hearty *ribollita*

Gourmets rather than gourmands, the Florentines like their food traditional and plain, without fancy sauces and condiments. Unsurprisingly, they creatively use bread in dozens of recipes. Three favorite lunchtime openers are *panzanella*, a bread "salad" made of moistened stale bread, fresh tomatoes and basil, and doused with olive oil, *pappa al pomodoro*, a bread soup made out of the same ingredients as *panzanella* but cooked, and *ribollita*, a bread soup made of bread, *cannellini* beans, cabbage, onion, garlic,

ripe tomatoes, and olive oil. Don't leave Florence without trying one or more of the delicious trio—you shouldn't have much trouble, since every good *trattoria* serves them. More uses of bread are detailed in "The Bread Report."

Legendary food shops and wine bars

Florence is not only a museum city. Walking around the historic center, you'll pass at least fifty shops that have been in business for over a century. Some of them carry delicious treats: Stop off at Procacci's on Via Tornabuoni for a celebrated truffles sandwich, sample the jams and rare teas at the Old England Store on Via Vecchietti, sip a hot chocolate in the elegant Caffè Rivoire established in 1872. For a simpler Florentine ambiance, try one of the tiny wine bars dotting the city, where you can enjoy a glass of wine and a sandwich. Two of the oldest and best known are located in Piazza dell'Olio and Via dei Cimatori.

core and outer sheath, was supported by a frame comprised of twenty-four ribs interconnected by a series of *"catene"* (reinforcements).

Giotto began work on the belltower in 1334, but died soon after the first level had been built. The project was continued by Andrea Pisano and completed by Francesco Talenti. The intense monumentality of the lower level gives way to the more decorative effect created by the three-part Gothic windows and geometrically patterned marble facing of the upper levels. The *bas-reliefs* along the lower level were sculpted by **Andrea Pisano** and **Giotto**. (The originals are in the nearby Museo dell'Opera del Duomo.)

The Museo dell'Opera del Duomo

The **Museo dell'Opera del Duomo** (Cathedral Museum) on the east side of Piazza del Duomo exhibits works originally designed for the Duomo, Baptistery, and Belltower, many of which are world-famous masterpieces. The best known is undoubtedly the *Pietà*, one of **Michelangelo's** last works (dated 1533), which was originally inside the Duomo. Vasari reports that the figure of the old man Niccodemus is a self-portrait. The *Virgin and Child* and seated portrait of *Boniface VIII* by **Arnolfo di Cambio** were sculpted for the Duomo facade, as were **Donatello's** *Prophets Jeremiah* and *Habakkuk*. The painted wood statue of **Mary Magdalene** originally stood in the Baptistery. Upstairs are the carved *Cantorie* (choir lofts) by **Donatello** and **Luca Della Robbia** from the Duomo, **Giotto** and **Pisano's** Belltower *bas-relief panels*, and the superb *silver altar* designed by **Michelozzo** and others for the Baptistery. Noteworthy is the exhibit of the tools and equipment used by Brunelleschi in building his dome.

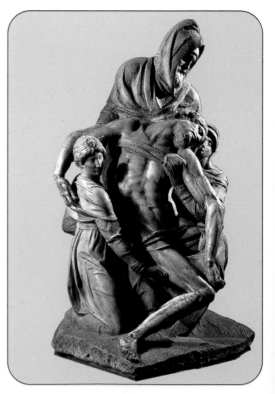

Wood statue *of* Mary Magdalene *by* Donatello (right) *and* Pietà *by* Michelangelo (far right)*, two of the masterpieces in the* Museo dell'Opera del Duomo.

For 700 years
the political heart of Florence

Palazzo Vecchio and Piazza della Signoria

Witness to the glories of the Republic, the martyrdom of Savonarola, the proclamation of the Plebiscite for the unity of Italy, but also to jesters, musicians, and merchants

Dominated by **Palazzo Vecchio**, **Piazza della Signoria** rises on the site of a Roman theater. It has been the political center of the city since the 14th century. Grandduke

Cosimo I de' Medici made it his "office building" in the 16th century when he moved his residence to the Pitti Palace. When the government offices were moved to the Uffizi (meaning "offices"), its designer Vasari, built an overhead passageway, now known as the **"Corridoio Vasariano,"** that crosses the Arno via Ponte Vecchio to connect the two palaces.

Florence's major political events took place in the square: Here, in 1498. **Fra Savonarola** was burned at the stake as a heretic. (The spot is marked by a round plaque in the middle of the square.) Here, in 1859, the Plebiscite by which the Grandduchy of Tuscany became part of the united Kingdom of Italy was announced.

Michelangelo's *David* has stood before Palazzo Vecchio as the symbol of Florentine liberty since 1504 (a copy; the original was moved to the Galleria dell'Accademia in the late 19th century). Sculptures adorning the square include the *equestrian statue of Cosimo I de' Medici* by **Giambologna** and the *Neptune Fountain* by **Ammannati** and **Giambologna**. Among the architectural highlights are the Gothic *Loggia dei Lanzi* (south side), **Palazzo Uguccioni**, attributed to Michelangelo or Raphael (north side), and the 14th century **Palazzo del Tribunale** di Mercatanzia (east side).

Palazzo Vecchio, *Florence's political center, Piazza della Signoria.* Left: courtyard *by Michelozzo,* Palazzo Vecchio. Below: bronze equestrian statue of Grandduke Cosimo I de' Medici *by Giambologna, Piazza della Signoria.*

Victory by Michelangelo (above left) *in the* Salone dei Cinquecento (above right). Below left: *Judith by Donatello in the* Sala delle Udienze, *Palazzo Vecchio.* Below right: Studiolo di Francesco I, *cryptic masterpiece in* Palazzo Vecchio.

Florence's civic center since the 13th century, **Palazzo Vecchio** is a simple rusticated stone building topped by crenelation and dominated by the tower rising 94 meters asymmetrically on the south side. It got its name *"vecchio"* (old) when the Medici moved their residence to the "new" Palazzo Pitti. It was modified by Cronaca (late 1400s) and Vasari (16th century).

Palazzo Vecchio is a treasure-trove of art marvels. On the ground floor is the frescoed *courtyard* designed by **Michelozzi**, in the center of which is a fountain adorned with a copy of **Verrocchio's** *Cupid*. Off the courtyard is the *Sala dell'Arme*, virtually intact since the 14th century.

On the second floor is the immense *Salone*

dei Cinquecento (Hall of the Five Hundred), commissioned by Fra Savonarola as a meeting hall for the Florentines elected to the Republican government.

The *frescoes* by **Vasari** are celebrations of Florence's military victories Tuscany, with a portrait of Cosimo I de' Medici the center. On the same floor is the *Sala dei Dugento* (Hall of the Two Hundred), a late 15th century work by **Benedetto da Maiano**, with a remarkable carved wood ceiling.

The striking *Studiolo of Francesco I*, the Medici prince's secret study, is richly adorned with paintings and a collection of art works and curiosities regarded as the origin of the modern museum. All the *historic apartments* (except for the mayor's offices) are open to the public, including the *Quartiere di Leone X*, whose chapel and rooms were frescoed by **Vasari** and his school, the *Quartiere degli Elementi* by **Giovanni Battista del Tasso**, and the *Quartiere di Eleonora of Toledo* (wife of Cosimo I de' Medici). Of special note in the Quartiere di Eleonora di Toledo are the *Gualdrada Room* and *Pietà* by **Bronzino** in the chapel. The *Sala dell'Udienza* (Audience Hall) is adorned with **Benedetto da Maiano's** carved *portal* and **Donatello's** bronze masterpiece of 1455, *Judith and Holofernes*. Other not-to-be missed sights are the *Sala dei Gigli* (Lily Hall), the *Sala del Mappamondo* (Map Room), and the *Cancelleria* (Chancellery),

Above: Perseus *by Benvenuto Cellini.* Left: Sala dei Gigli, Palazzo Vecchio. Below: *aerial view of the* Loggia dei Lanzi, *Piazza della Signoria.*

which was once the office of Niccolò Machiavelli (represented by a portrait bust). On the mezzanine are fifteen rooms teeming with masterpieces, including statuary from Antiquity (the *Lancellotti Discobolus*, a Roman copy of Myron's original and a statue of *Aphrodite*), Renaissance paintings (*Madonna dell'Umiltà* by **Masolino da Panicale** and a *Virgin* attributed to **Masaccio**), as well as works by Bronzino, Tintoretto, Rubens, and Hans Memling. There is also a fascinating collection of musical instruments.

Built around 1380 by Benci di Cione and Simone Talenti for public ceremonies, the loggia on the south side of the square is a veritable sculpture museum. It is known by three names: *Loggia della Signoria*, *Loggia dell'Orcagna* (after the architect), and, most commonly, *Loggia dei Lanzi* (because it was the gathering place for the German mercenaries known as Lanzichenecchi). The facade is adorned with reliefs of *Virtues* by **Agnolo Gaddi**; the free-standing statues include the *Rape of the Sabines* and *Hercules and Nessus* by **Giambologna**; *Menelaus and Patroclus*, a Roman copy of a Greek original; the *Rape of Polyxena*, a 19th century work by **Pio Fedi**; and six *Roman female figures*. On the west corner is **Benvenuto Cellini's** masterpiece, *Perseus* with the head of Medusa (1546-1554). The incredible craftsmanship of the Michelangeloesque Mannerist statue and the elaborate base reveal Cellini's origins as a goldsmith.

And, for dinner, *trippa* and beans

Traditionally, Florentine cuisine is not meat-based. Among the meat dishes, *trippa* (cow's stomach cut into thin strips and cooked with carrots, onions, and abundant tomato sauce) and *lampredotto* (boiled cow's interiors) represent its proletarian origins better than the aristocratic **bistecca alla fiorentina**. Outdoor stalls in the historic center still offer **trippa** and **lampredotto**, served hot in sandwiches.

One of Florence's best known dishes is **cannellini** beans. They are cooked in dozens of different ways, including in the most traditional manner inside a glass flask.

The Neptune Fountain and the "Biancone"

One of Florence's outstanding monumental fountains is the Neptune Fountain which Bartolomeo Ammannati designed and sculpted for Cosimo I de' Medici between 1563 and 1575.

The white marble statue of Neptune (called "Il Biancone" by the Florentines) on a seahorse-drawn chariot is believed to be a portrait of Cosimo. Giambologna and Ammannati sculpted the graceful figures of the satyrs and nymphs.

According to legend, Ammannati was so remorseful about having sculpted such daring nudes (for the times!) that he was plagued by insomnia for years.

The Bargello, the treasure-trove of Italian sculpture

Below: David by Donatello (left) and David by Verrocchio (right).

Tino di Camaino, Verrocchio, Donatello, Michelangelo, Cellini: masterpieces in marble, stone, and bronze from the Early Renaissance to the High Renaissance

The forbidding castle known as the Bargello was originally built in the 13th century as the headquarters of the governors, Capitano del Popolo and Capitano di Giustizia, and the police chief, Bargello. Later, it served as a dungeon: Public executions were carried out in the courtyard and the corpses of those put to death were hung from the windows as a warning to the populace. A sculpture museum since 1865, it is regarded as Italy's foremost collection of Renaissance sculpture.

Masterpieces of pre-Renaissance sculpture include the *Virgin and Child* by **Tino da Camaino** (13th century), the solemn *Virgin and Child with Sts. Peter and Paul* by **Paolo di Giovanni** (14th century), the *Coronation*

The invention of ice cream

According to tradition, ice cream was invented by Florentine Bernardo Buontalenti in the 16th century. Buontalenti, who worked as an architect and designer under the grand-dukes, was in great demand for creating fabulous entertainments for

the court parties—his fireworks and water spectacles were legendary. Today, Florence is still famous for its great ice creams. An incredible array of flavors and varieties can be enjoyed in the numerous ice cream specialty shops around town.

of Ferdinand I of Aragon by an unknown Florentine master (15th century).

Among **Michelangelo's** masterpieces on display on the ground floor are the youthful *Drunken Bacchus*, the bust of the Roman hero, *Brutus*; and the so-called *Pitti Tondo* with the Virgin and Child with St. John. Several celebrated works are displayed on the second floor, including Benvenuto Cellini's trial casting for Perseus and a winged *Mercury* and the *Davids* by **Verrocchio** and **Donatello**.

Donatello's bronze *David* wearing only a wide-brim hat, commissioned by Cosimo the Elder, is the first nude of the Renaissance. Other remarkable 15th century sculptures are a portrait bust in marble of the *Florentine merchant Francesco Sassetti* by **Antonio Rossellino**, *Lady with a Bouquet* by **Verrocchio**, and *St. George* by **Donatello**, as well as glazed *terracottas* by **Andrea** and **Luca Della Robbia**.

Left: Pitti Tondo *by Michelangelo.*
Far left: Lady with a Bouquet *by Verrocchio.*
Above: *courtyard of the* Bargello.

Historic soccer

The oldest Florentine sport is historic soccer, which became popular in the 15th century. Today, games are held in Piazza Santa Croce on June 24, the feast-day of the city's patron saint, St. John the Baptist, and on June 28, the feast-day of Sts. Peter and Paul. The games are preceded by a parade of Renaissance dames, mounted knights, pages, and foot soldiers. Four teams, each representing one of the historic Florentine districts (Santa Croce, Santo Spirito, San Giovanni, Santa Maria Novella), compete for the prize, which consists of a painted **palio** (banner) and a live white calf. Historic soccer resembles American football and British rugby more than contemporary soccer, since the ball is played with the hands (and other parts of the body, as physical attacks are allowed).

A game lasts fifty min-

utes, and must not end in a tie. There are twenty-seven players on each team, four of whom are goalies. A cannon shot is sounded whenever a **"caccia"** (point) is scored.

The Uffizi Gallery, probably the world's oldest and best known museum

In 1560, Cosimo I de' Medici commissioned **Vasari** to build the **Uffizi** (offices) to house the Grandduchy's offices, courts of laws, and state archives.

The Medici's immense art collection was transferred to the Uffizi by Cosimo's son and successor, Grandduke Francesco I, who commissioned **Bernardo Buontalenti** to add the octagonal *Tribuna*.

In 1737, the last of the Medici, Anna Maria Luisa, donated the collec-

tion to the City on the condition that it would never be dismembered and that no part of it would ever be removed from Florence.

At the end of the 18th century, Grandduke Pietro Leopoldo modernized the Uffizi, separating the art and science collections.

The quality and the quantity of its collections make the Uffizi, the world's oldest museum and one of its finest.

A – Entrance hall
B – First corridor
C – Second corridor
D – Third corridor
E – Entrance to the *Corridoio Vasariano*
F – Buontalenti's Staircase - Exit
G – Terrace overlooking the Loggia dell'Orcagna
1 – Antiquity *
2 – Giotto, Cimabue, Duccio
3 – 14th century Sienese painting
4 – 14th century Florentine painting *
5/6 – International Style
7 – Early Renaissance
8 – Filippo Lippi
9 – Antonio del Pollaiolo
10/14 –Botticelli
15 –Leonardo
16 – Map Room *
17 – Hermaphrodite Room
18 – The *Tribuna*
19 – Perugino and Signorelli
20 – Dürer and the German school
21 – Giovanni Bellini and Giorgione
22 – Northern European school
23 – Correggio
24 – Miniatures *
25 – Michelangelo and his school
26 – Raphael and Andrea del Sarto
27 – Pontormo and Rosso Fiorentino
28 – Titian and Sebastiano del Piombo
29 – Parmigianino and Dosso
30 – Emilian school
31 –Veronese
32 –Tintoretto
33 – Corridor of the 16th century school
34 – Lombard school
35 – Barocci *
38 – Buontalenti's Vestibule *
41 – Rubens *
42 – Niobe and her children
43 – Caravaggio *
44 – Rembrandt *
45 – 18th century school *

(* Currently not open to the public)

Plan of the Uffizi

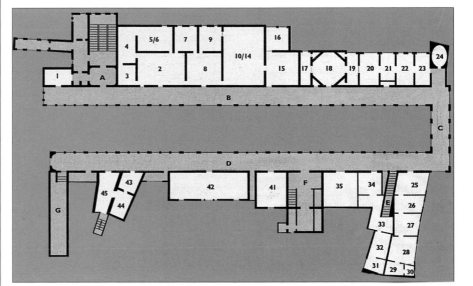

And now
the "Grandi Uffizi"

The "Grandi Uffizi," or expanded Uffizi, has been planned to meet the demands of the ever-increasing number of visitors, who topped one million in 1999.

The revamped museum will have increased exhibition space (from 7000 to 30,000 square meters), with ninety new rooms doubling the number of works on display from 2000 to 4000), an enlarged museum shop, and a new library.

The displays will be updated to provide visitors with a better understanding of the historic progression of the works on exhibit.

Last but not least, a grandiose new entranceway will be opened on Via Castellani, which is currently the rear part of the east wing.

Doni Tondo
by Michelangelo.

Facing page above:
night view of the Piazzale degli Uffizi.
Below: portrait
of Cosimo de'
Medici *by Pontormo.*

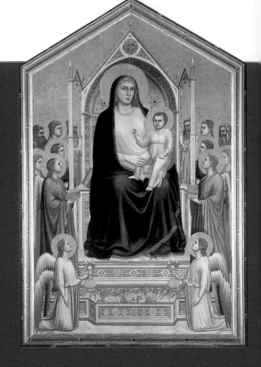

Galleria degli Uffizi: the history of Italian painting and much more

Simply listing the major works of art in the Uffizi would be a Herculean task. Just consider that, among the many, many other celebrated masterpieces, there are fifteen Botticellis, three Leonardo, and two Caravaggios. Exhibited are the seminal works from the major schools of Italian painting, starting from Florentine and Sienese masters (Cimabue, Giotto, and Duccio di Boninsegna).

In addition to works by Flemish masters such as Hugo van der Goes and Rubens and Spanish masters such as Velàzquez and Goya, the Uffizi collections include Greek and Roman statues, miniatures, and tapestries.

There are also dozens of self-portraits contributed by artists from the 16th century to our day (e.g., Chagall and Guttuso), some of which are hanging in the **Corridoio Vasariano**.

The **Gabinetto dei Disegni e delle Stampe**, the Uffizi print and drawings collection, is

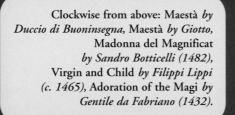

Clockwise from above: Maestà *by Duccio di Buoninsegna,* Maestà *by Giotto,* Madonna del Magnificat *by Sandro Botticelli (1482),* Virgin and Child *by Filippi Lippi (c. 1465),* Adoration of the Magi *by Gentile da Fabriano (1432).*

Clockwise from above:
Allegory of Spring *by
Sandro Botticelli
(1482-1483),* Virgin of
the Goldfinch *by Raphael
(1506),* Birth of Venus
*by Sandro Botticelli
(1484-1486).*

Annunciation *by
Leonardo da Vinci
(c. 1470),* Self-Portrait
by Diego Velàzquez
(below right), Flora
by Titian (c. 1515)
(below far right).

unique in its field.

The *Maestàs* by **Cima-bue**, **Giotto**, and **Duc-cio** in the first room are the starting point from which all Italian painting originated.

The following rooms display masterpieces of the Sienese school by masters such as Simone Martini and the Loren-zettis and the International Style by masters such as Gentile da Fabriano.

The Early Renaissance is represented by, among others, **Masaccio** *(Virgin and Child with St. Anne)* and **Botticelli**; the High Renaissance, by **Miche-langelo** *(Doni Tondo),* **Leonardo** *(Annuncia-tion),* and **Raphael** *(Virgin of the Goldfinch).* There are also works by Luca Signorelli, Perugino, and splendid portraits by Bronzino.

The Venetian school is represented by Mantegna, Giorgione, Titian, and Tintoretto, with a whole room dedicated to Veronese.

The Northern European school is represented by Lucas Cranach, Dürer, Holbein the Younger, and Hans Memling.

There are also masterpieces by **El Greco** and **Caravaggio** (Bacchus, *Sacrifice of Isaac,* and *Medusa).*

Last, but not least, there is a room dedicated to Rembrandt.

The princes' passageway runs over the river and through the garden...

The **Ponte Vecchio** rises on the site of a Roman bridge and its numerous successors, all of which were destroyed in flooding of the Arno River. It is the only Florentine bridge to have emerged unscathed from the German bombs of World War II. Built in 1345, possibly by Neri di Fioravante or Taddeo Gaddi, it was lined on either side by butcher shops until 1591, when the butchers were evicted and replaced by jewelers. In the center is a *bust of Benvenuto Cellini*, Florence's most illustrious goldsmith.

The **Corridoio Vasariano**, built in 1564 by **Vasari** as a special passageway between the Uffizi and the Pitti Palace for the Medici, is the second floor of Ponte Vecchio. The recently

Above: Palazzo Pitti. Below: *the connection between* Palazzo Vecchio *and the* Palazzo Pitti. *The area inside the figure formed by* Palazzo Vecchio, Palazzo Pitti, Fortezza da Basso, *and* Forte Belvedere *was controlled by the Medici granddukes.* Facing page: Boboli Garden (above), Grotto *by Bernardo Buontalenti*, Boboli (center), *and* Ponte Vecchio (below).

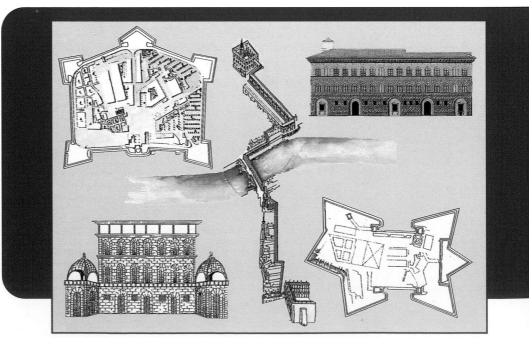

restored **Corridoio** is adorned with sculptures and the Uffizi's *self-portrait collection.*

We come out at Florence's biggest palace, **Palazzo Pitti**, which was commissioned in 1457 by the merchant Luca Pitti, who demanded that his dwelling be bigger and more sumptuous than that of his rivals, the Medici. Brunelleschi designed the original core consisting of the seven central windows. The Medici bought it out in the mid-1500s. The wings (known as *"rondò"*) were added under the Lorraine grandukes in the 17th century. Today, seven museums are housed in the palace.

In 1550, Eleonora of Toledo, Cosimo I de' Medici's wife, commissioned architect-sculptor Niccolò Pericoli, known as **Tribolo**, to

landscape the palace gardens (today called **Boboli**). His artful combination of flower beds and lawns interspersed with grottoes, fountains, and statuary became the prototype of the formal Italian garden. Among the most noteworthy sights are the *Grotto* by **Bernardo Buontalenti** (16th century), *Venus* by **Giambologna** (16th century), the *amphitheater of Verzura* (remodeled in the 18th century), and the *Giardino del Cavaliere* near the Museo delle Porcellane.

Two great galleries: Palatina and Arte Moderna

The Pitti Palace's two great museums, the Galleria Palatina (Palatine Gallery) and the Galleria d'Arte Moderna (Museum of Modern Art), are totally different, but equally fascinating. The Palatina collection was founded in the 17th century by the last of the Medici granddukes and continued by their successors, the Lorraines. It is displayed in great halls, splendidly decorated by **Pietro da Cortona** with *allegorical frescoes celebrating the Medici.* First open to the public in the 19th century, it was later completed with works on permanent loan from the Uffizi. Hung according to its creators' whims rather than modern museum criteria, it is a fascinating example of a private collection reflecting the tastes of those who built it. Among its celebrated masterpieces are works by **Raphael** (*Madonna della Seggiola, Madonna del Granduca,* and *La Velata* and the *wedding portraits of Agnolo and Maddalena Doni*) and by **Titian** (*The Concert, Portrait of Pietro Aretino,* and *Man with a Glove*). There are also masterpieces by **Botticelli** (*Portrait of a Lady*), **Fra Bartolomeo** (*Deposition*), **Filippo Lippi** (*Virgin*), **Andrea**

Facing page: Portrait of a Lady *by Sandro Botticelli* (above left), Madonna della Seggiola *by Raphael* (above right), The Concert *by Titian* (center)

This page: La Velata *by Raphael* (above left), Mary Magdalene *by Titian* (above right), The Three Ages of Man, *16th century* Venetian school (center)

del **Sarto** (*Assumption of the Virgin* and the *Holy Family*), and **Caravaggio** (*Sleeping Cupid*). Among the Northern European masterpieces are *Ruben's Four Philosophers* and the *Consequences of War*, as well as *portraits* by **Van Dyck**.

Founded in 1860, the *Galleria d'Arte Moderna* is a collection of 19th and 20th century Italian school works. On display are works by **Giovanni Duprè**, **Stefano Ussi**, **Giuseppe Bezzuoli**, **Xavier Fabre**, and **Antonio Canova**. In addition, there are paintings by **Giovanni Fattori** and **Telemaco Signorini** of the **Macchiaioli** (contemporaries of the French Impressionists), portraits by **Giovanni Boldini**, and sculpture by **Adriano Cecioni**.

Two Pitti museums, the **Carriage Museum** *and the* **Costume Museum**, *are especially fascinating. Don't miss the* **royal apartments** *on the second floor, which were, in chronological order, the residence of the Medici princes, the Lorraine granddukes, and the Savoy royal family. Among the sights are the sumptuous* **Throne Room**, *the* **Sala Bianca** (*White Room*), *and the* **Sala Verde** (*Green Room*). *The rooms housing the* **Museo degli Argenti** (*Silver Museum*) *on the ground floor were frescoed by Giovanni di San Giovanni. The collection consists of heirloom jewelry, inlays with gemstones, enamels, glassware, and cameos, that once belonged to the Medici and Lorraine granddukes. Of special note are Lorenzo the Magnificent's semiprecious stone vases, 17th century German carved ivories, the treasury of the Salisburg bishops, and a celebrated lapis-lazuli vase.*

Dining room, royal apartments, (below left), Fisherman, German, Silver Museum (below right).
Singing Together *by Silvestro Lega*, Galleria d'Arte Moderna.

Michelangelo's David and Pietà

Above: David *by Michelangelo*. Right: *interior of the Galleria dell'Accademia*. Below: Slave *by Michelangelo*.

The Galleria dell'Accademia was built in 1784. Among its celebrated masterpieces are Michelangelo's David, Pietà, and Slaves, and paintings by Botticelli and Perugino.

The Michelangelo sculptures in the Galleria dell'Accademia (Academy Gallery) represent all stages in the master's *oeuvre*. The *David* of 1504 is a youthful work, the four unfinished *Slaves* carved for the tomb of Pope Julius II in Rome are works of his maturity, and the *Palestrina Pietà* is one of his last works. Today, people from all over the world come especially to see the David, the very embodiment of Renaissance ideals. The statue is innovative in several respects: David is depicted as an adult and not as a young boy, he is nude and not clad in armor, and he is shown about to go to battle and not emerging victorious. Because the statue was meant to be viewed from below, his head and heavily veined right hand appear unduly oversize.

The *Pietà* and the *Slaves* represent pure emotion captured in stone. The highlights of the painting collection are a *crucifix* attributed to **Duccio**, an *altarpiece* by **Orcagna**, two *Virgins* by **Botticelli**, and Giambologna's plaster model for the sculpture of the Rape of the Sabines in Piazza della Signoria.

Tomb of Giuliano, Duke of Nemours, with Day and Night (left) *and* Lorenzo, Duke of Urbino, with Dawn and Dusk (right) *by* *Michelangelo,* Sagrestia Nuova.
Center: Virgin and Child *by* *Michelangelo,* Sagrestia Nuova.
Below: Cappella dei Principi *by Matteo Nigetti.*

The Medici Chapels

The Medici Tombs that Michelangelo made famous

1534. At the foot of the commemorative statues are the celebrated figures of *Day* and *Night* (on Giuliano's sarcophagus) and *Dawn* and *Dusk* (on Lorenzo's sarcophagus). Above the sarcophagus at the far end containing the remains of Lorenzo the Magnificent and his brother Giuliano is **Michelangelo's** superb *Virgin and Child with Sts. Cosmas and Damian.*

The *Medici Tombs,* which belong to the architectural complex of the Basilica of San Lorenzo, consist of the *Cappella dei Principi* (Princes' Chapel) and the *Sagrestia Nuova* (New Sacristy). The sumptuous *Cappella dei Principi,* whose dome resembles the Duomo's, was begun in 1602 by **Matteo Nigetti** on a commission from Grandduke Ferdinando I. Work on the facing of colored marbles and semiprecious stones proceeded for over a century. Six granddukes are buried in the elaborate sarcophagi.

Pope Clement VII, born Giulio de' Medici, commissioned **Michelangelo** to build the so-called *New Sacristy* (to distinguish it from **Brunelleschi's** *Old Sacristy*), the burial place of Giuliano de' Medici, Duke of Nemours, Lorenzo the Magnificent's third son, and Lorenzo, Duke of Urbino. Michelangelo worked on the project between 1520 and

Above left:
Crucifixion with St.
Dominic *by Fra
Angelico*, San Marco.
Above right:
Annunciation *by Fra
Angelico*, San Marco.

*Masterpieces
of the San Marco Museum*

Fra Angelico's
mystic mystery

and frescoes adorn the halls and cells of the monastery.

Among the masterpieces by the mystical friar-painter are the *Annunciation*, *Noli Me Tangere*, *Transfiguration*, and *Coronation of the Virgin* and, in the Ospizio dei Pellegrini, the *Deposition* and *Last Judgment*.

Center right:
Chiostro di
Sant'Antonino, *a
cloister by
Michelozzo.*
Below: Last Supper
by Andrea del Sarto,
San Salvi.

Commissioned by Cosimo the Elder, the **monastery of San Marco**, including the *cloister of Sant'Antonino* and the *library*, was designed by **Michelozzo** in the 15th century. Many famous men lived here, including the prior-bishop of Florence, St. Antonino; the Dominican reformer friar, Girolamo Savonarola, who was burned at the stake as a heretic in Piazza della Signoria in 1498; and Fra Angelico, whose paintings

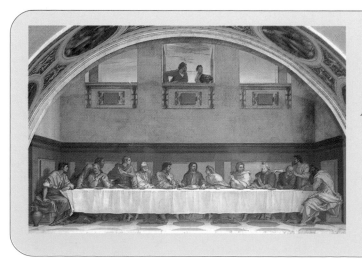

THE LAST SUPPER was the typical subject for decorating the walls of monastery dining halls (refectories). Florence has some splendid examples: the 14th century renditions by Taddeo Gaddi in Santa Croce and Orcagna in Santo Spirito, the 15th century ones by Andrea del Castagno in Santa Apollonia and Ghirlandaio in the church of Ognissanti, and the 16th century one by Andrea del Sarto in San Salvi.

The Archeological Museum

Antiquity from Etruria to Egypt

Palazzo della Crocetta, built in 1620, is Florence's *archeological museum*. There are three major collections: Etruscan civilization, the Etruscan-Greek-Roman Antiquarium, and Egyptian art. Among the celebrated works of the Etruscan collection, which was started by Cosimo the Elder, are the *Chimera* excavated in Arezzo (5th century B.C.), the *Mater Matuta* (5th century B.C.), the *Haranguer* (3rd century B.C.), and the *François Vase*, a black figure vase dating from the Attic period.

The Egyptian collection, Italy's most important after the Egyptian Museum of Turin, comprises sarcophagi, funerary urns, and a wooden chariot from the necropolis of Thebes. Outstanding among the sculptures are a statue and a painted *relief of the cow goddess Hator* and a *funerary statuette of the priest Amenemhet.*

Masterpieces from the **Archeological Museum***: bronze* **Chimera, Etruscan,** *4th century B.C.* **(above left), François Vase, Attic,** *4th century B.C.* **(above center), Mater Matuta, Etruscan,** *5th century B.C.* **(above right).** *From the* **Science Museum: worktable (below left)** *and* **Galileo's lens (below right).**

Galileo at the Science Museum

The **Museo della Storia della Scienza** *(History of Science Museum) in Piazza dei Giudici near the Uffizi, is one of the world's major science museums.*
The highlight is Galileo's collection of instruments, including his lenses and viewing glasses. On display are medical, surgical, chemical, and pharmaceutical instruments and equipment, measuring devices, and mechanical constructions.

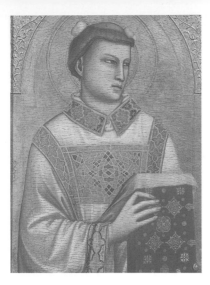

Two collectors, one English, Herbert Percy Horne, and one Florentine, Stefano Bardini, donated their marvelous collections to the city in the early 19th century. The **Horne Museum**, located in a 15th century palace on Via de' Benci, has an outstanding collection of sculpture, furnishings, and paintings, the most celebrated of which is **Giotto's** *St. Stephen*. Among the other important works are a sculpture of the *Virgin* by **Antonio Rossellino**, a *Virgin with Saints* by **Lorenzo Monaco**, and a *Holy Family* by **Beccafumi**.

The **Bardini Museum** was open to the public in 1923 in Palazzo dei Mozzi just across the river from the Horne Museum. The highly personal private collection consists of sculpture, paintings, and weapons, dating from Antiquity to the 18th century, as well as antique furnishings and tapestries. Sculptural highlights include a *Woman's Head* by **Nicola Pisano**, *Charity* by **Tino di Camaino**, and the *Madonna dei Cordai* by **Donatello**. In addition, there are *Virgins* by followers of **Ghiberti** and **Jacopo della Quercia**.

The **Stibbert Museum** was donated to the City of Florence by the 19th century Anglo-Florentine collector,

Above: St. Stephen *by Giotto*, Museo Horne (left), Madonna della Scala *by Michelangelo*, Casa Buonarroti (center), Cavalcade, Museo Stibbert. Below: *interior of the* Museo Marino Marini.

Minor museums—minor in size, but not in quality

Frederick Stibbert, whose main interest was arms and armor. His extensive collection is still housed in his neo-Gothic mansion situated in the northern part of the city. One of the most popular exhibits is the *Cavalcata*, consisting of life-size mounted figures clad as medieval knights. The museum has recently been reorganized and expanded to better display the eclectic collection, ranging from Flemish paintings to musical instruments, which are exhibited in the Salone dell'Armeria, Sala della Malachite, and the huge Salone-Galleria.

The **Casa Buonarroti** is situated in the attractive 15th century building Michelangelo bought for his nephew, which was later remodeled by his grandnephew, Michelangelo Buonarroti the Younger. A museum since 1858, it has an important collection of Michelangelo's works, including sculptures and drawings. The sculptures, all early works, comprise two marble relief carvings, the *Madonna della Scala* (Virgin of the Stairs) and the *Battle of the Centaurs*, and a wooden *crucifix*, which is believed to have been sculpted for the church of Santo Spirito. Paintings attributed to Paolo Uccello and Titian are also on display.

Below: inlaid table, *1878,*
Opificio delle Pietre Dure.
Bottom: Charity *by Tino di Camaino,* Museo
Bardini (left), *photo from* Alinari *archive* (center),
and Cityscape *by Filippo De Pisis (1931),*
Alberto Della Ragione Collection (right).

A one-of-a-kind museum, the **Opificio delle Pietre Dure** (precious and semiprecious stone works) was founded in 1588 by Ferdinando I de' Medici and restructured in the 18th century by Grandduke Pietro Leopoldo as a workshop for Florentine craftsmen specialized in the art of *"commesso,"* i.e., mural designs in semiprecious stones cut in such a way as to give the impression of being a picture. Today, the Opificio is as an important restoration center. On display are superb examples of *commessi.*

Florence also has museums and collections of modern and contemporary art. The **Museo Marino Marini**, dedicated to Marino Marini (b.1901-d.1980) was opened to the public in 1988 in the unconsecrated church of San Pancrazio. On display are 177 of the master's works, including bronzes, stone carvings, paintings, drawings, and engravings with the recurrent Marini motifs of horse and rider and sensuous female figures.

Like the American Kodak Museum of Rochester and the German Agfa Museum of Cologne, the **Museo Storico della Fotografia Fratelli Alinari** is an invaluable photo archive. Started in 1855 by the renowned photographers, brothers Leopoldo, Giuseppe, and Romualdo Alinari, it now contains over 600,000 negatives and 150,000 photos dealing mainly with Italian art, city- and landscapes, and portraits.

Having seen the Alinari photos of Florence in the 19th and 20th centuries, you will be inspired to make a visit to the **Museo Firenze Com'era** (Museum of Florence As It Once Was). On display are historical maps, prints, drawings, and documents.

Special interest museums include the **Musical Instruments Collection**, which is located inside the Conservatorio Luigi Cherubini (music school) and the prestigious **Alberto Della Ragione Collection of 20th Century Italian Art**, which Alberto Della Regione donated to the city in 1970.

PALAGIO DEI CAPITANI DI PARTE GUELFA

14th century – Characterized by an unusual exterior stairway, Palagio dei Capitani di Parte Guelfa was the headquarters of the powerful Guelph magistrates.

PALAZZO DEL BARGELLO

1255 – The headquarters first of the Capitano del Popolo (governor) and then of the *Bargello* (police chief), Palazzo del Bargello was for centuries used as a prison; today, it is one of Italy's major sculpture museums.

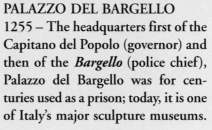

Stones and Money

THE HISTORY AND EVOLUTION OF THE GREAT FLORENTINE PALACES

PALAZZO DAVANZATI

14th century – One of the best preserved of the 14th century palaces, Palazzo Davanzati is now the Museo dell'Antica Casa Fiorentina (Museum of the Historic Florentine Home).

PALAZZO MEDICI-RICCARDI

1444-1460 – An Early Renaissance masterpiece by Michelozzo, Palazzo Medici-Riccardi was commissioned by Cosimo the Elder and served as the Medici residence for several generations.

PALAZZO ANTINORI

1461-1466 – A simple, elegant, design with overhanging eaves, Palazzo Antinori has been attribuited to Giuliano da Maiano.

PALAZZO CORSINI

Late 17th century – Overlooking the Arno, Palazzo Corsini was designed by stage designer Anton Maria Ferri in a style influenced by the Roman Baroque architect, Borromini.

The stately palaces of Florence, with their rusticated stone facades, graceful courtyards, and priceless art, embody the power and glory of the city between the 14th and 18th centuries. Here are some outstanding examples.

PALAZZO STROZZI

1489 – One of the most distinctive Renaissance palaces, Palazzo Strozzi was commissioned by merchant Filippo Strozzi and designed by Benedetto da Maiano and Cronaca.

PALAZZO PITTI

1457 – Acclaimed as one of the great palaces of Europe, the Pitti Palace was commissioned by merchant Luca Pitti and designed by Brunelleschi. Today it houses seven museums.

PALAZZO RUCELLAI

1446-1451 – Designed by Leon Battista Alberti, Palazzo Rucellai was designed for the Rucellai family whose descendants still inhabit it. It is celebrated for its patterned marble facade.

Historical palaces and cafés

Some of Florence's greatest palaces—and some of its greatest coffee bars—are situated on fashionable streets such as Via Maggio and Via Tornabuoni. One of the most exclusive, *Caffè Giacosa*, opened in 1905, is on Via Tornabuoni. Three more are located in nearby Piazza Repubblica. *Caffè Giubbe Rosse* (literally, red jackets, from the color of the waiters' uniforms) has been the meeting place for Florentine intellectuals since the turn of the century. Across the way are *Caffè Paszkowski*, whose customers are serenaded by a live orchestra, a favorite with politicians, and *Caffè Gilli*, renowned for its refined Art Nouveau ambiance.

Great and noble craftsmen

Many a stately Florentine palace conceals the fervent activity of a high fashion atelier. For over fifty years, fashion designer and **Marchese** (marquis), **Emilio Pucci** and now his daughter, Laudomia, have represented Florentine high fashion from their residence-atelier in Palazzo Pucci. The Ferragamo atelier is in Palazzo Feroni on Via Tornabuoni where Salvatore **Ferragamo** founded his shoe empire decades ago. Gucci, another Florentine fashion leader, is also headquartered in a Via Tornabuoni palace.

Above right: Museo dell'Antica Casa Fiorentina (Museum of the Historic Florentine Home), Palazzo Davanzati. Below: Journey of the Wise Men by Benozzo Gozzoli, chapel of Palazzo Medici-Riccardi.

STATELY AND OVERPOWERING, YET HARMONIOUS and graceful, the Florentine **palazzi** lining the tiny streets of the medieval city represent a true triumph of stone over space. The princely palaces, with their elegant loggias, portals, and simple facades, symbolize the wealth and power of the great Florentine merchant and banking families.

The 13th century **Bargello**, now a museum, is illustrated on page 34.

Palagio dei Capitani di Parte Guelfa, built in the 14th century and remodeled by Brunelleschi in the 15th century and Vasari in the 16th century, is characterized by an unusual external staircase. **Palazzo Davanzati**, one of the finest examples of 14th century Florentine architecture, was restored at the turn of the century by antiques dealer Elia Volpi. Now a museum (**Museo dell'Antica Casa Fiorentina**), it has a fascinating collection of home furnishings, linens, and kitchen utensils from the 14th to the 17th centuries. Among the highlights are the *Wedding Chamber* and two frescoed rooms (the *Sala dei Pappagalli*, Parrot Room, and the *Sala dei Pavoni*, Peacock Room). **Palazzo Medici-Riccardi**, the prototype of the Florentine Renaissance palace, was commissioned by Cosimo the Elder and served as the Medici residence until 1540. **Michelozzo's** striking *facade* is divided into three distinct registers, the first faced in rough stone, the second in rusticated stone, and the top one in planed blocks. The corner windows on the ground

floor level, called *"inginocchiate"* (kneeling windows) are ascribed to Michelangelo. Inside is the *chapel* frescoed by **Benozzo Gozzoli** in 1459-1460 with a scene ostensibly showing the *procession of the Wise Men on their way to Bethlehem*, which is actually a glorification of the Medici family. (Lorenzo the Magnificent, for example, is portrayed as a youth on horseback.) The elegant **Palazzo Antinori** is still the residence of the family renowned for its wine. Take advantage of the old Florentine tradition of selling wine in palaces and stop off for a drink at the *Cantinetta Antinori* on the ground floor. Commissioned by merchant Giovanni Rucellai, **Palazzo Rucelli**, with its striking geometric pattern facade, was designed by **Leon Battista Alberti** and built by **Bernardo Rossellino**. **Palazzo Pitti**, Florence's biggest palace, is illustrated on page 40.

Perhaps the finest example of Florentine Renaissance architecture extant, **Palazzo Strozzi** was commissioned by merchant Filippo Strozzi. The project was begun by **Benedetto da Maiano** and completed by **Cronaca**, who is responsible for its distinctive cornice. Its elegant effect is achieved by a rusticated stone facing with wrought-iron ornaments by Caparra.

The building is occupied by the *Gabinetto Vieusseux*, a library and foundation specializing in 19th century Italian history. The 17th century **Palazzo Corsini**, whose elaborate facade is reflected in the Arno River it overlooks, is one of the rare examples of Florentine Baroque.

Built on the site of a 4th century Early Christian basilica, **San Lorenzo** was commissioned by the Medici and designed by **Brunelleschi**. Its facade was never completed. The interior is in Brunelleschi's hallmark understated style. Off the south transept is the *Sagrestia Vecchia* (Old Sacristy, in contrast to Michelangelo's New Sacristy), also designed by **Brunelleschi** and decorated by **Donatello**. The interior of the church is adorned with masterpieces of sculpture (**Donatello's** two *bronze pulpits* and the *marble tabernacle* by **Desiderio da Settignano**) and painting (*Marriage of the Virgin* by

Left: *unfinished facade of* San Lorenzo; *nave of* San Lorenzo (above).

From the historic center to the Oltrarno

THE GREAT FLORENTINE CHURCHES

Rosso Fiorentino and *Annunciation* by **Filippo Lippi**).

The *Laurentian Library*, entered by way of the cloister, was designed by **Michelangelo** in the early 16th century to house a superb collection of codexes and illuminated manuscripts. Originally built in 1250 as a sanctuary dedicated to the Virgin, **Santissima Annunziata** was remodeled by **Michelozzo** and **Leon Battista Alberti** in the 15th century. The outer porch was added in the 1500s.

Especially noteworthy are the two cloisters: the *Chiostrino dei Voti* with *frescoes* by **Andrea Del Sarto**, **Pontormo**, and **Franciabigio** and the *Chiostro dei Morti* in the adjoining monastery with Mannerist school frescoes. Inside the church is a much venerated image of the Virgin Annunciate, that was painted in the 14th century by an unknown Florentine master. Other highlights include paintings by **Andrea del Castagno** (*Christ and St. Julian* and the *Trinity*). The **church of San Marco**, situated next to the San Marco monastery and museum (page 46), has an 18th century facade. The interior was remodeled by Giambologna and Silvani. Inside is a superb 13th century crucifix in the style of Giotto.

Tempietto *by Michelozzo.* Santissima Annunziata *with Brunelleschi's* Ospedale degli Innocenti (center), *and 18th century* facade *of* San Marco (below).

Santa Croce,
Franciscan glory

Santa Croce, Florence's great Franciscan church, was designed by Arnolfo di Cambio in 1294. Like Westminster, it is a burial place for famous Italians. (The 19th century Italian poet Ugo Foscolo, who is buried in the church, wrote a famous poem about the tombs titled *I Sepolcri.*) All together, there are 276 tombs: from relief floor slabs to free-standing monuments.

The most noteworthy are, artistically speaking, the *tombs of Leonardo Bruni* by **Rossellino** (1444) and *Carlo Marsuppini* by **Deside-** **rio da Settignano** (1453) and, historically speaking, of Machiavelli (1784), Vittorio Alfieri by Canova (1810), Gioacchino Rossini, and Galileo.

Among the many masterpieces are the carved *pulpit* by **Benedetto da Maiano** (third pier on the right) and the *Madonna del Latte* (Virgin of the Milk) by **Rossellino**. The chapels are a veritable museum of 14th century fresco painting: *Cappella Peruzzi* and *Cappella Bardi* were frescoed by **Giotto** with scenes from the lives of St. John the Baptist (Peruzzi)

and St. Francis (Bardi); *Cappella Castellani* was frescoed by **Agnolo Gaddi**; *Cappella Baroncelli* was frescoed by **Taddeo Gaddi**. A superb *crucifix* carved by **Donatello** in 1425 is hanging in one of the chapels.

The *sacristy* is decorated with frescoes by **Taddeo Gaddi**, **Spinello Aretino**, and **Niccolò Gerini**. At the south side of the church is the entrance to the cloisters. At the far end of the *Primo Chiostro* is the *Pazzi Chapel*, one of the most celebrated masterpieces of Renaissance architecture, which **Brunel-**leschi started in 1443. Entering the chapel from the outer portico composed of six Corinthian columns and a *frieze of cherub heads* by **Desiderio da Settignano**, you find yourself in pure Brunelleschi space.

As always, the rhythmic, harmonious effect is enhanced by the contrast of gray *pietra serena* against the white walls. Glazed terracotta tondos by Luca Della Robbia are the sole adornment. The second cloister, *Chiostro Grande*, is also based on a Brunelleschi design.

Above: sacristy, Santa Croce (left) *and the crucifix by Cimabue that was damaged in the 1966 flood* (right).

Below: Pazzi Chapel *by Brunelleschi: interior* (left) *and exterior* (right).

Santa Maria Novella: facade *by Leon Battista Alberti* (left) *and interior* (right). Below: Nativity of the Virgin *by Domenico Ghirlandaio* (left) *and* Trinity *by Masaccio* (right).

Santa Maria Novella, Dominican glory

Work on Santa Maria Novella, Florence's great Dominican church, started in 1246. The facade was begun in the 14th century: the lower part is in the Tuscan Romanesque-Gothic style, while the upper part, completed by **Leon Battista Alberti** in the 15th century, is a masterpiece of the Early Renaissance style. The Gothic arches (known as *"avelli"*) on the street side are actually tombs. Inside, on the left aisle wall is **Masaccio's** fresco of the *Holy Trinity*, which ranks as one of his greatest works.

The chapels of Santa Maria Novella are filled with masterpieces: *Cappella Rucellai* with a *Virgin* by **Nino Pisano** and the *tomb of Leonardo Dati* by **Ghiberti**: *Cappella di Filippo Strozzi* frescoed by **Filippo Lippi**, which contains the *tomb of Filippo Strozzi* by **Benedetto da Maiano**; *Cappella Maggiore* with **Ghirlandaio's** frescoes with scenes from the life of the Virgin; and *Cappella Gondi* with **Brunelleschi's** only wood sculpture, a *crucifix*. Another *crucifix*, believed to be a youthful work by **Giotto**, is hanging in the *Sacristy*.

The cloisters are not to be missed: in the *Chiostro Verde* (Green Cloister) are *frescoes* by **Paolo Uccello** and in the *Cappellone*

degli Spagnoli (literally, Chapel of the Spaniards, because it was the meeting place of the Spanish entourage of Eleonora of Toledo) are 14th century *frescoes* glorifying the Dominican order by **Andrea Bonaiuti**.

Orsanmichele and Santa Trinita

Orsanmichele, situated between the Duomo and Palazzo Vecchio, rises on the site of a grain storehouse built by Arnolfo di Cambio in 1284 that burnt down in a fire. The elegant Gothic building was designed by **Francesco Talenti** and **Neri di Fioravanti** in the 14th century. The outer facades are decorated with *tabernacles*, each of which contains the coat-of-arms and statue of the patron saint of the guild that commissioned it. The statues constitute a compendium of 15th century sculpture: *Sts. John the Baptist and Matthew* are by **Ghiberti**, *St. George* by **Donatello** (a copy; the original is in the Bargello) and *Four Saints* by

Nanni di Banco. Inside is the *tabernacle* by **Andrea Orcagna**, a masterpiece of Gothic architecture and craftsmanship. The panel painting of the *Virgin* in the tabernacle was painted by **Bernardo Daddi** in 1347.

Originally built in the 11th century, **Santa Trinita** has a striking 16th century *facade* designed by **Buontalenti**. Inside are *frescoes* by **Ghirlandaio** (*Cappella Sassetti*, right transept), a panel *painting* by **Lorenzo Monaco** (fourth chapel on the right), a wooden *statue of Mary Magdalene* by **Desiderio da Settignano**, and the *tomb of Federighi* by **Luca Della Robbia**.

The *Rificolona* Festival

Florentines—especially kids—have always loved the *Rificolona* Festival, which is held on the Virgin's feast day, September 8, and thus traditionally associated with the holy image of the Virgin in the church of Santissima Annunziata. Each celebrant carries his/her *rificolona* (candle-lit lamp made of colored paper) on a long pole. Originally, the festivities, accompanied by much bell-ringing and eating of *brigidini* cakes, were held to Piazza dell'Annunziata, but today the festival takes place on and along the Arno River, with music and dancing in the glow of the *rificolone*.

Above: Orsanmichele: *exterior* (left) *and interior with* Orcagna's Tabernacle (right). Left: Santa Trinita: Adoration of the Shepherds *by Domenico Ghirlandaio and* facade (far left).

Santo Spirito was started by **Filippo Brunelleschi** and completed by his pupil, **Antonio Manetti**. The interior, in Brunelleschi's typical harmonious style, is characterized by the striking visual effect of the columns that sweep the eye to the dome-crowned crossing.

Among the noteworthy sights are the Baroque *main altar* by **Giovanni Caccini** (1608), a painting of the *Virgin and Child with Donors* by **Filippo Lippi** (1490), and an altarpiece with the *Virgin and Child with Saints* by **Maso di Banco**. Not to be missed are the *Cap-*

Santo Spirito, Santa Maria del Carmine, and Masaccio

Above: Santo Spirito: facade (left) *and* nave *by Brunelleschi* (right)
Below: Santa Maria del Carmine: facade (left) *and* Expulsion from Paradise *by Masaccio,* Brancacci Chapel.

Sweet things on the Florentine table

In addition to the traditional Tuscan sweets (illustrated in this guide), Florence has some special ones of its own. Most are seasonal: In the fall, everyone eats **schiacciata con l'uva** (grape cake), a sweet bread baked with the newly harvested grapes; during Carnival, **schiacciata alla fiorentina**, a plain cake made of flour, eggs, sugar, and lard topped with confectioner's sugar; and around March 19 (St. Joseph's feast-day, and thus Italian father's day), **frittelle di riso**, fried rice balls. An eternally popular dessert in Florence is **castagnaccio** (a flat cake made of chestnut flour) which is described in "The Chestnut Report." Another favorite dessert is **zuccotto**, which is a kind of ice cream cake. **Pan di ramerino**, which is sold in bakery shops all over Florence, is a kind of spicy bread. Read more about traditional breads and baked goods in "The Bread Report."

pella Corbinelli designed by **Sansovino** in the late 15th century and the superb *Sacristy* designed by **Giuliano da Sangallo**.

Behind the plain facade of **Santa Maria del Carmine**, founded in the 13th century, is one of the great masterpieces of Western painting: the *frescoes* painted in 1425 by **Masaccio** (1401-1428) in the *Brancacci Chapel*. Miraculously, the Brancacci Chapel and the nearby *Corsini Chapel* (designed by Silvani and Fog-

portant International Style painter, was commissioned by the Florentine merchant, Felice Brancacci to fresco the Brancacci family chapel. Masolino, forced to abandon Florence, left the project to his protégé, Masaccio, who worked on it until his death, after which it was completed by **Filippino Lippi**. Masaccio innovatively treated space and color, using realism to convey the impact of the Biblical stories. The scenes painted by Masaccio are the *Expulsion*

gini and frescoed by **Luca Giordano**) emerged unscathed from the fire that destroyed much of the church in 1771. Originally, **Masolino da Panicale**, Masaccio's master and an im-

from Paradise, *The Tribute Money*, and *St. Peter Baptizing*, *The Temptation of Adam and Eve* is by **Masolino**, and both artists worked on *St. Peter Resurrecting Tabitha*.

San Miniato al Monte: patterns of marble and gold

Dedicated to the 4th century martyr, St. Miniato, the Romanesque **church of San Miniato al Monte** scenically overlooks the city from a hilltop. It has a distinctive green and white facade with a 13th century *mosaic of Christ enthroned between the Virgin and St. Miniato.* Atop the facade is an eagle, the symbol of the church's caretaker, the Calimala guild.

The interior has a typically Romanesque plan, with a raised choir and lowered crypt at the east end. At the end of the nave, which is paved with a marvelous 13th century mosaic floor, is the *Cappella del Crocifisso* designed by **Michelozzo** in 1448 and decorated with glazed *terracottas*

by **Luca Della Robbia**. The *Cappella del Cardinale del Portogallo* (chapel of the Cardinal of Portugal, Jacob of Lusitania, who is buried inside), designed by **Antonio Manetti**, is a remarkable example of the Early Renaissance style. Among the highlights are the *cardinal's tomb* carved by **Rossellino**, an *Annunciation* by **Baldovinetti**, and *Angels* by **Antonio** and **Piero del Pollaiolo**.

Frescoes by **Taddeo Gaddi** adorn the crypt ceiling. The great mosaic in the apse representing *Christ enthroned with the Virgin and St. Miniato* dates from the 13th century. The **sacristy** is decorated with late 14th century *frescoes* of scenes from the life of St. Benedict by Spinello Aretino.

San Miniato: facade (above) *and* St. Benedict *by Spinello Aretino* (center). Below: chapel of the Cardinal of Portugal *with the* sarcophagus *of the cardinal by Antonio Rossellino* (right) *and* mosaic of Christ Enthroned, *apse of* San Miniato (far right).

Piazzale Michelangelo, Forte Belvedere, and the Cascine

Panoramas and promenades

The winding Viale dei Colli, "one of the loveliest drives in Italy" according to the Italian Tour Association, and **Piazzale Michelangelo** *were built by the Florentine architect Giuseppe Poggi between 1870 and 1873. Piazzale Michelangelo affords a breathtaking view of Florence and beyond to the hilltown of Fiesole. Built as a museum, the* **Loggia** *on the highest terrace is now an elegant restaurant-café. In the center of the square is a bronze copy of Michelangelo's David.*

Scenic **Forte Belvedere**, *commissioned by Ferdinando I de' Medici in 1590, was designed by* **Bernardo Buontalenti**. *A marvel of military engineering, it is used for exhibitions and festivals.*

The green that stands out in the cityscape of Florence is the **Parco delle Cascine** (*literally, pastureland park) where the Medici cattle once grazed. The* **Ghiacciaia Pyramid**, **Narcissus Fountain**, *and the* **Le Pavoniere** *complex were built in the in the 18th century when it was turned into a public park.*

Above: David *(a bronze copy of Michelangelo's marble statue) in Piazzale Michelangelo.* Below: Forte Belvedere *by Bernardo Buontalenti.*

The magnificent environs of Florence

Fiesole, Certosa, and Pratolino

First Etruscan and then Roman, **Fiesole** is situated on a hilltop overlooking Florence. The major sights are the Romanesque **Duomo** (1028), the **Museo Bandini**, with works by the Della Robbia, Taddeo and Agnolo Gaddi, and Lorenzo Monaco; and the 15th century **Palazzo Pretorio**. Don't miss the **Roman Theater** and **Archeological Museum** exhibiting locally excavated ceramics and bronzes. In the summer, the Roman Theater, which seats three thousand, is used for live performances and film festivals.

Located five kilometers from the city center in the town of Galluzzo, the **Certosa** (chartreuse) of Florence was founded in 1341 by Niccolò Acciaioli. Its chief attraction is the recently restored fresco cycle of scenes of the *Passion of Christ* by **Pontormo**. Other noteworthy sights are the Cloisters, the Refectory, the Pharmacy, and the remarkable 16th century carved choir stalls in the church of San Lorenzo.

The **Pratolino Park**, situated on the old road to Bologna, is all that remains of the villa designed by Bernardo Buontalenti for Francesco I de' Medici in the 16th century and purchased in the 19th century by the Demidoff family. Originally, there were fountains, water falls, grottoes, and pools everywhere. Now, all that remains of the original design is the gigantic (19 meters tall) *allegorical figure of the Apennine* modeled by **Giambologna**.

Above: facade *of the* church of San Francesco *(14th-15th centuries), Fiesole.* Center: gigantic statue of Apennine *by Giambologna,* Villa di Pratolino. Below: *Certosa di Galuzzo: view of monks' cells.*

The magnificent environs of Florence

The Chianti region from Impruneta to Greve

The countryside of the **Chianti** region, where Tuscany's great wines are grown (described in "The Wine Reports"), with its harmonious patchwork of vineyards and olive groves accented with farmhouses, castles, and cypresses, is unique in the world.

The town of **Impruneta** grew up around a sanctuary dedicated to the Virgin. A church, the basilica of **Santa Maria dell'Impruneta**, was built on the spot in the 11th century. The outer portico was added in the 17th century; the belltower, in the 13th century. Inside are Della Robbia glazed terracottas, a fine 14th century Florentine school altarpiece, and the Byzantine image of the Virgin, still much venerated today.

The history of **Greve**, one of the delightful towns situated in the heart of the Chianti region, goes back to the Middle Ages. The town center, and site of the annual Chianti Wine Festival, is a charming asymmetrical main *square* bordered by porticoes. In the **church of Santa Croce**, which was remodeled in the 19th century, are two important paintings: the 15th century *Altarpiece of the Annunciation* by **Bicci di Lorenzo** and a *Virgin with Saints* painted by the **Master of Greve** in the 13th century. There is also a superb glazed terracotta *Deposition* group in the nearby **Oratorio di San Francesco**.
Nearby is the enchanting little hilltown of **Montefioralle**, where Amerigo Vespucci was born.

Above: *Montefioralle, the birthplace of Amerigo Vespucci* (left) *and the* facade *of the* basilica of Santa Maria, *Impruneta* (right). Below: *main square of Greve.*

The magnificent environs of Florence

The Medician Mugello of Borgo San Lorenzo, Vicchio, and Scarperia

Some call the Mugello Valley, the birthplace of the Medicis, Giotto, and Fra Angelico, an isolated and quiet place, others call it a mystic place. Starting from **Barberino di Mugello** (along the Autostrada del Sole) and following the Sieve River, we arrive at the picturesque Franciscan monastery of Bosco ai Frati, which Michelozzo designed in the early 15th century. Inside are two *crucifixes*, one by **Donatello** and another attributed to **Desiderio da Settignano**.

Passing **Cafaggiolo**, the site of one of the Medici villas, and **San Piero a Sieve**, with its 16th century Fortezza di San Martino designed by Buontalenti, we reach **Scarperia**. Since the 16th century, Scarperia has been renowned for its fine cutlery. Once there were over fifty workshops in the town; most of the smaller ones have shut down in recent years. There is a fascinating **Museum of Knives** and a Cutting Instrument Trade Fair held every two years. Other highlights include the **Palazzo Pretorio** and the **Oratorio della Madonna di Piazza**, both situated on the main square.

Borgo San Lorenzo, the capital of the Mugel-

lo, is a busy agricultural and industrial center. Don't miss the 12th century **church of San Lorenzo** and the 18th century **Oratorio dei Miracoli**.

Vicchio is the birthplace of two great artists; **Fra Angelico** and **Giotto**. The 13th century fortifications are still visible in the town's structure.

Dicomano, an agricultural and industrial center, was founded by the Etruscans. If you order a glass of wine, you'll no doubt be served one of the fine Chiantis produced in nearby Rufina or Pontassieve.

Above: *monastery of* Bosco ai Frati (left) *and view of Scarperia* (right). Below: monument to native *son Giotto, Vicchio.*

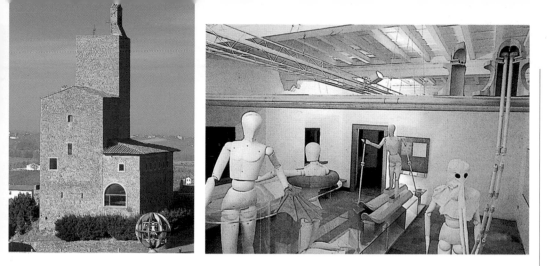

The magnificent environs of Florence

In the footsteps of Boccaccio and Leonardo: Vinci, Empoli, Certaldo, and Vallombrosa

Leonardo's birthplace **Vinci** still preserves its intensely scenic setting of olive groves and vineyards, as well as numerous reminders of its native son. The major sights include the **Leonardo da Vinci Museum**, with exhibits of models built from Leonardo's designs and facsimiles of his notebooks, and the **Leonardo da Vinci Library**, which caters to the needs of Leonardo scholars from all over the world. You can visit the **church of Santa Croce** where Leonardo was christened and the *house* in nearby **Anchiano** where he was probably born in 1452.

Certaldo, the birthplace of **Boccaccio**, is not far from Vinci. The reconstructed *Boccaccio House* is now occupied by a foundation, the Centro Nazionale di Studi. Noteworthy are the 13th century **church of Santi Michele e Jacopo** and the 15th century **Palazzo Pretorio**, whose exterior has numerous coats-of-arms and whose interior is richly frescoed. **Empoli**, one of the area's major agricultural and industrial centers, has some fascinating historical sights, including **Palazzo Ghibellino** and the **Collegiata Church**, whose museum has a *Pietà* by **Masolino da Panicale**. Deep in the forest is the **abbey of Vallombrosa**, which is described in "The Monastery Report."

Above: *Vinci:* castle of Count Guidi (left) *and the* Leonardo da Vinci Museum (right).
Below: church of Santa Maria a Ripa, *Empoli* (left) *and* Giovanni Boccaccio's house, *Certaldo* (right).

Tuscany: land of great wines

Seventy thousand hectares of vineyards cultivated since Etruscan times, export of fine wine since the Renaissance–in Tuscany, wine-making is a science and an art.

Tuscany is probably just as famous for its wines as it is for its art treasures and scenic wonders. Today, eighty thousand wine producers produce four billion liters of wine on a territory covering seventy thousand hectares of vineyard. The earliest

Above: Bacchus *by Caravaggio*, Uffizi. Right: *wine festival in Renaissance costume.*

Tuscan wine producers were the Etruscans and the Romans, to whom wine was sacred. After the fall of the Roman Empire the vineyards lay fallow until the year 1000, when wine-making was resumed in the abbeys and towns of Tuscany. In 1282, during a period of great prosperity

Wine in the world

Thirty billion liters of wine is produced annually worldover, with slightly more than half (15.5 billion) produced in the European Union alone. Around 95% is consumed in the industrialized countries. The world's largest consumers are Italy (with sixty liters per capite annual consumption) and France. The United States consumes two billion liters, or 7.9 liters per capite. Argentina and Chile are growing exporters.

The hard physical labor of the past centuries called for nutritious food and drink that could rapidly be transformed into energy, and this made the working classes great wine consumers. Today, insufficient calo-

production, consumption, and exportation expanded to an incredible extent. Lorenzo the Magnificent, who was a talented poet as well as a ruler, sang the praises of wine in verses fittingly titled "The Triumph of Bacchus and Arianna." In the 18th century, the celebrated Accademia dei Georgofili, the agriculture institute founded in Florence and still operating as a foundation, conducted research into developing scientific methods for wine cultivation and production. In the 19th century, famous Tuscans such as Bettino Ricasoli and Raffaello Lambruschini were among the first to produce wine according to the modern criteria. These many centuries of experience have contributed to the fame and fortune that Tuscan wines enjoy today.

and growth, the wine guild was founded in Florence. About the same time, *osterie* (taverns) became popular all over the region. Wine was popular with the working classes and the aristocrats alike. Not only was it appreciated for its taste, but it was also believed to be a source of energy and a remedy for a host of diseases.

During the 15th and 16th centuries, at the height of the Tuscan Renaissance, wine

Above: *views of the celebrated Tuscan landscape.* **Below:** *beer is the drink in Germany.*

rie intake is no longer a problem and, in addition, consumer habits have changed as a result of campaigns against drinking alcoholic beverages and, more recently, incessant advertising in favor of beverages such as beer and soda. Therefore, since wine is no longer regarded simply as a source of calories, but rather as one of the pleasures of the good life, quality, as opposed to quantity, has become the main concern of wine producers.

When all is said and done, wine, consumed in moderate quantities, is a healthy beverage, a boon to socialization, and a link to our past.

The legendary wine flask

The use of glass in Tuscany dates back to the Etruscans. By the 13th century, master glassblowers were producing all kinds of glassware. The term "flask" to indicate the long stemmed, wide-bodied glass containers commonly used throughout Europe probably derives from the Gothic *"flasko."* The popular wine flask with the straw bottom originated in the mid 1400s. Production was the responsibility of the *fiascai*, who gathered grass along the

banks of the Arno and dried it for the *"sala,"* as the straw bottom is called.

The flask has been in use for centuries (as shown by the woman carrying a flask in the detail from Ghirlandaio's 15th century fresco of the Nativity of the Virgin in the church of Santa Maria Novella reproduced here) and, for many reasons, including hygiene, is still regarded as the best container for wine and olive oil.

The great Chianti wines

The Chianti region, famous for its wine and agriturismo *vacations, is divided into seven production zones. Its heart is the hilly region lying between Florence and Siena.*

Chianti stands for Italian wine par excellence—and indeed wine has been produced in this area since time immemorial. Today, the Chianti territory covers a vast area of Tuscany and the term "Chianti" has also come to indicate the production method which was developed and codified by statesman-agronomist Baron Bettino Ricasoli in the 19th century.

The Chianti region is divided into seven zones. Chianti, which produces 140 million liters of wine annually is Italy's largest territory with Doc *(Denominazione di origine controllata)* and Docg *(Denominazione di origine controllata e garantita)* certification. The Chianti Classico region

covers seventy thousand hectares of hilly territory between Florence and Siena, producing the prestigious Chianti Classico wine. The others, **Montalbano**, **Rufina**, **Colli Senesi**, **Colli Fiorentini**, **Colline Pisane**, and **Colli Aretini**, all produce fine Doc wines. Excellent wines are also produced in the outlying area comprising

Montespertoli, **Cerreto Guidi**, **Agliana**, **Gambassi**, and **San Miniato**.

Even though the grapes for all Chiantis are the same (Sangiovese, black Canaiolo, Trebbiano, and Malvasia), some wines are headier, and thus well suited to aging, while others have less body, and thus should be enjoyed young.

Rules of wine and noses

Rule 1: Never serve two wines of similar alcoholic content or aging at the same meal.
Rule 2: Serve wines in order of strength, starting from the lightest (young) to the strongest (aged), from white, rosé, to red.
Rule 3: Don't serve more than two or

The three wine kings

BRUNELLO DI MONTALCINO. Brunello di Montalcino, one of the world's great wines, is produced in a tiny area of 24,000 hectares south of Siena. It comes from a single variety of grape, the Sangiovese grosso. Not much of it is produced and what there is of it is exceedingly costly. Locally known in the 16th century, by the 17th century it was already in demand by foreign connoisseurs—William III of England, for example, imported it for his table. In 1980, it became Italy's first Docg wine. Brunello, aged to perfection, is the perfect accompaniment to elaborate dishes such as game, stews, and cheeses...or to peaceful meditation on long winter evenings.

VINO NOBILE DI MONTEPULCIANO. In the 17th century, the physician-poet Francesco Redi dubbed Vino Nobile di Montepulciano the "king of wines" ("Montepulciano d'ogni vino è il re"). Granite colored and with an aroma of violets, it is produced in an area of 24,000 hectares. It is a hearty wine that traditionally accompanies equally

Facing page: *wood casks for aging wine* (above) *and flask transport wagon* (below).
This page: *San Gimignano* (above), *Montepulciano with* Palazzo Tarugi *and* Palazzo Contucci (right) *and Montalcino* (right).

three wines at a single sitting.
In cooking with wine, use the same wine you will later serve at the table. Use young wines to add flavor and tenderness to meats and aged wines to give zest to sauces and soups. Only white wines should be added to rice dishes.

hearty main courses such as roast dishes.

VERNACCIA DI SAN GIMIGNANO. Known since the 13th century, Vernaccia di San Gimignano is a fine white wine made of a single grape, the Vernaccia, and produced in an area covering 38,000 hectares. Doc certified, it is a golden colored dry wine with a delicate aroma. It is popular as an apertif and is often drunk with seafood dishes.

Enoteche, wine shrines

Tuscan wine producers have become more and more quality conscious as wine connoisseurs take over from wine guzzlers. In the past, Tuscany was filled with **fiaschetterie** (wine bars), where people would stop off during the day for a glass of wine. Later came the **bottiglierie** (wine and liquor stores) where wines and liquors were sold in sealed bottles. Today, many prefer the **enoteche** (wine boutiques) where they can taste great wines and sometimes eat a superb meal as well. The renowned **enoteche** of Florence, Siena, and San Gimignano are stocked with all the finest Italian and imported wines, including the great Tuscan red wines, white wines from Trentino and Friuli, as well French wines and champagnes.

More fine wines

The white and red wines produced in the hilltowns around Lucca and the Isle of Elba are a fitting complement to the local specialties.

Above: *sommelier selecting a wine.*
Right: *Tuscan table setting.*

From the great estates of the hills surrounding Lucca come fine wines: both red (*Rosso delle Colline Lucchesi*) and white (*Bianco delle Colline Lucchesi*). Both have been Doc certified: The Rosso, one of the first Italian wines to receive Doc certification, was certified in 1968, and the Bianco was certified in 1985.

The **Isle of Elba** has been renowned for its red and white wines since the famous naturalist Pliny the Elder defined it the "fertile island of wine" two thousand years ago. The sea air renders Elban wines unique in aroma and taste. Elban white wines are made from Trebbiano grapes, whereas the red wines, which are never aged more than three years, are made from the Sangiovese isolano variety.

Dessert wines are coming back. *Moscadello di Montalcino*, a Doc dessert wine produced from Moscato bianco, is a delicious recent revival.

Another fine Doc wine is fragrant *Morellino di Scansano*, produced from the Sangiovese grape, and aged to 11.5 degrees. It is a perfect complement to the hearty specialties of its native Maremma region.

Tuscany's over twenty Doc wines cover barely forty percent of the region's total grape production. The rest become *"vini da tavola"* (table wines), whose alcoholic content never exceeds 10.5 degrees, but whose quality is often excellent. Outstanding are the red wines of the **Colli dell'Etruria Centrale** such as *Cardisco*, *Biturica*, *Muschio*, and *Selvante*.

White wines

Famous for its red wines, Tuscany also produces some extraordinary white wines. One of the best is **Bianco di Montecarlo**, a smooth, dry, pale yellow wine, which is produced in small quantities south of Lucca. Other fine white wines are **Bianco della Valdinievole** (produced between Pescia and Montecatini), **Bianco di Pitigliano**, **Bianco Pisano di San Torpé**, **Bianco Vergine Val di Chiana**, **Bianco di Bolgheri**, and **Candia dei Colli Apuani**.

Left: *wine harvest.*
Below: *bunches of grapes left on reeds for vinsanto production.*

Vinsanto, the traditional hospitality wine

Vinsanto (literally, holy wine) is traditionally offered to pilgrims and guests in the Tuscan countryside. Dry, semidry, or sweet with a minimum alcoholic content of 17 degrees, it is delicious alone or with desserts. It is made from green grapes sun-ripened on vines with southern exposure that, after harvesting, are dried for months on straw or reed beds. The fermented grapes are then aged for a minimum of three years in *"caratelli"* (small oak casks) in special storerooms appropriately known as *"vinsantaie."*

Tuscany produces 100,000 liters of Doc and 300,000 of regular vinsanto annually. The seven Tuscan Doc *vinsanti* are *Bianco della Valdinievole, Bianco Pisano di San Torpé, Carmignano, Colli dell'Etruria Toscana, Montescudaio, Pomino,* and *Val d'Arbia.*

Build your own wine cellar

Building a wine cellar for your fine wines is both pleasurable and useful. It should be located in a cool, dry, well-aired spot—remember wine is a living substance that needs to breathe. It

should have a capacity of at least one hundred horizontally positioned bottles. For the best preservation, spumante bottles should be stored upside down near the floor. White wines should be placed on top of the **spumante**. Red wines should be placed on top of the white wines in order of aging (with the longest aged on top). The main serving recommendations are: White wines should be cooled in the refrigerator some hours before serving and red wines should be opened at least an hour before drinking. Aged wines should be served in a carafe so that thel full aroma is liberated.

THE MEDICI VILLAS

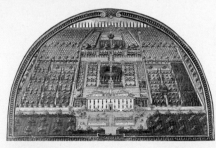

● Above: Medici villa *at Poggio a Caiano.*
Center: *16th century lunette painting of a Medici villa by Justus Utens.*
Below: Villa Ferdinanda, *Artimino.*

Between the 15th and 16th centuries, the Medici built sumptuous residences all over Tuscany, many of which have come down to us virtually intact. Among these are the **Villa di Careggi** designed by **Michelozzo** near Florence and the **Villa di Cafaggiolo** and **Villa del Trebbio** in the Mugello Valley. Perhaps the most splendid is the **Villa di Poggio a Caiano**, near Pistoia, which **Giuliano da Sangallo** built for Lorenzo the Magnificent in 1480. Its highlights are the apartments of Bianca Cappello, mistress of Francesco I de' Medici, who mysteriously died here in 1587, and the **Salone Centrale**, the great hall frescoed by the Mannerist masters **Alessandro Allori**, **Andrea del Sarto**, and **Pontormo**. Of great elegance is the **Villa La Ferdinanda at Artiminio** near Carmignano, which was designed in the late 1500s by **Bernardo Buontalenti** as a hunting lodge for Ferdinando I de' Medici. Since hunting was practiced even in winter, each room has a fireplace, which is why there are so many chimneys protruding from the roof. Other noteworthy villas are the **Villa di Castello** between Florence and Prato, the **Villa Ambrogiana** at Montelupo, and the **Villa La Petraia** and **Villa di Lappeggi** in the environs of Florence.

PRATO

The symbol of Prato, the second most populous city in Tuscany, is the majestic **Castello dell'Imperatore** (above) named after Emperor Frederick II, who commissioned it around 1250. The marble-faced square building, with its distinctive corner towers and Ghibelline crenelation, was never finished, and was only later joined to the city walls. In summer, visitors can enjoy open air performances inside the spacious courtyard and panoramic views of the city from the battlements.

Prato's civic center is the **Palazzo Comunale**, which was originally built in the 13th century and remodeled in the neo-Classic style in the late 1700s. In the atrium is the *Fontana del Bacchino* (Bacchus Fountain) sculpted by **Ferdinando Tacca** in 1656, one of the city's most beloved monuments. Copies of the fountain can also be found on the square and in the facing brick and stone Gothic building, **Palazzo Pretorio**, which is now the **Museo Civico** art museum.

The popularity of the "relic of the Holy Gir-

A renowned textile-trading center since the Middle Ages, Prato is where the bill of exchange was invented. Yet, at the same time, it has always been an art center, famous for its medieval buildings, Fra Filippo Lippi paintings, and the Museo d'Arte Contemporanea, one of Italy's major collections of contemporary art.

Above: Emperor's Castle, c. 1250.

Below: Bacchus Fountain *by Ferdinando Tacca, 17th century* (left) *and the* Virgin and St. Thomas *by Filippo Lippi* (right).

dle" motif in the churches of Prato is a sign of the city's deep devotion. The Holy Girdle which, according to legend, was donated St. Thomas by the Virgin, was taken from Jerusalem to Prato in the 12th century by the merchant, Dagomari.

The Holy Girdle Reliquary is preserved in the **Duomo**, which was founded before the year 1000 and built in the 13th century. On the right side of the facade is the *Pergamo del Sacro Cingolo* (pulpit of the Sacred Girdle) sculpted by the 15th century masters, **Donatello** and **Michelozzo**. Inside is the *Capella del Sacro Cingolo* (chapel of the Sacred Girdle) built for the reliquary and decorated with 14th century *frescos* with *Stories of the Relic* by **Agnolo Gaddi**. On the altar is a bust of the *Virgin and Child* sculpted by **Giovanni Pisano** in 1317. In a chapel north of the choir is the late 15th century *tomb of Filippo Inghirami*, attributed to **Benedetto**

Above: facade *of the* Duomo *with the* pulpit *carved by* Donatello and Michelozzo *visible on the right side.*

Cantucci, cantuccini, *and, of course, almonds*

Prato has a sweet tooth, especially for almonds. The city's most popular dessert is the Mantovana, *based on a recipe created by two pilgrim nuns from Mantua, whose main ingredients are a mixture of flour, butter, eggs, and sugar, topped by a layer of chopped almonds. Almonds are also a prime ingredient of* bruttiboni *(literally, bad looking, good tasting), cookies*

made of almond paste with sugar, eggs, whites, and lemon peel - which appeared out of nowhere sometime in the last century and which have been disappearing down people's throats ever since. The most popular Pratese *cookies, however, are the* cantucci di Prato, *the culinary masterpiece of 19th century pastry chef, Antonio Mattei, whose shop on Via Ricasoli is still selling them. Shaped like little yellow bridges, the* cantucci *are made of flour, sugar, yeast, eggs, salt, and, of course, almonds. Variations can be made with orange peel or anise.*

Francesco Datini, medieval entrepreneur, inventor, and benefactor

Francesco di Marco Datini (b. 1330-d. 1410), the inventor of the bill of exchange a precursor of the Renaissance Humanist and the modern-day entrepreneur, created a huge trading empire, which from Prato branched out all over Europe. He brought prosperity to his hometown by opening it up to trade with Pisa, Genoa, Avignon, Majorca, and Spanish ports. When he died, he left his immense fortune of 70,000 gold florins to the poor and all his papers to posterity. A commemorative statue of the great man, wearing a round hat and a long cloak and holding a bill of exchange, stands before the Town Hall. The nearby Palazzo Datini *contains an archive (above) of Datini's personal and business correspondence, as well as a collection of historic textiles. The kings and queens who once were guests here have long since been replaced by scholars from all over the world.*

Three symbols of Prato: Francesco Datini (above), Teatro Metastasio (below left), and a smoke stack (below right).

da Maiano, after a prototype by Bernardo Rossellino.

Among the city's most noteworthy religious monuments are the 13th century **church of San Francesco** with its Tuscan Romanesque striped facade, the 13th century **church of Sant'Agostino**, and the majestic **church of San Domenico**, with its distinctive arcading and a frescoed *Sala Capitolare*. Perhaps the most renowned of Prato's churches is **Santa Maria delle Carceri**, designed in 1485 by **Giuliano da San Gallo**, in a style recalling that of Filippo Brunelleschi. The interior is adorned by terracottas by **Andrea della Robbia** and works attributed to **Francesco da San Gallo**.

PAINTINGS BY FILIPPO AND FILIPPINO LIPPI IN PRATO MUSEUMS.

Since **Filippo Lippi** and his son **Filippino Lippi** lived and worked in Prato for many years, it is hardly surprising that several of their masterpieces are still preserved in the city.

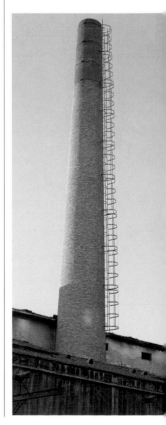

Among the famous works by Filippo Lippi in Prato are the remarkable fresco of *Herod's Banquet*, from a cycle in the *Capella Maggiore* in the **Duomo**, the *Burial of St. James Altarpiece* in the **Museo dell'Opera del Duomo**, and the *Virgin Handing Her Girdle to St. Thomas* in the **Museo Civico**. Filippino Lippi's *Virgin and Child*, now on exhibit in the Museo Civico, originally adorned the tabernacle in Piazza Mercatale.

Church of Santa Maria delle Carceri *by Giuliano da Sangallo (1485) (right) and* Burial of St. Stephen (detail) *by Filippo Lippi,* Duomo (far right).

Masterpieces by other artists include the seven original panels from **Donatello's** *pulpit* and the *reliquary of the Holy Girdle* (Museo dell'Opera del Duomo), *Stories of the Holy Girdle* by **Bernado Daddi**, *altarpiece* by **Giovanni da Milano** (Museo Civico), and *Christ with Angels* by **Volterrano** (**Museo di Pittura Murale** in the church of San Domenico).

Prato musts

Nobody who comes to Prato, the town that has been dealing in textiles and textile machines for over seven centuries, should leave without a visit to the *Museo del Tessuto* (Textile Museum) in Palazzo del Comune, which exhibits a fascinating collection of 15th-18th century fabrics and models of looms.

Several famous Italians, including Atto Vannucci, Gabriele D'Annunzio, and contemporary novelist, Tommaso Landolfi, either studied or taught at the *Convitto Nazionale Cicognini*, which was founded by the Jesuits in 1699 and turned into a state school in the 19th century. Its most interesting features are the dining room and theater.

If you can stay overnight, make sure to reserve a seat at the *Teatro Metastasio* which hosts Italy's top theatrical companies. The building's neo-Classic facade was designed around 1830 by Luigi Cambray Digny.

THE LUIGI PECCI MUSEUM, PRATO'S SHOWPLACE OF CONTEMPORARY ART.

The Luigi Pecci Museum, *Prato's 12,000-meter-square showplace of contemporary art, was opened to the public in 1988. Donated to the city by native son, Enrico Pecci, it exhibits works by Cucchi, Merz, Albert Hien, and Anne and Patrick Poirer. The museum comprises an Education Center, a Documentation Archives, and a performance hall.*

Left: Banquet of Herod *by Filippo Lippi (1452-1465)*, Duomo.
Below: open-Air Museum *of* Villa di Celli, *Pistoia:* Horse *by Marino Marini* (left) *and* Jupiter's Thunder *by Anne and Patrick Poirier.*

PEOPLE FROM ALL OVER come to admire the fresco of Herod's Banquet, *that* Filippo Lippi *painted as part of the St. John the Baptist cycle in the Duomo. Accustomed to sacred Last Suppers, or* Cenacoli, *a common subject in Florentine painting, art-lovers cannot help feasting their eyes on the profoundly profane banquet set before them by Filippo Lippi.*

Art and nature in Celle

Art patron-collector, Giuliano Gori, opened his collection to the public in 1982. It is set in an 18th century estate, Celle, that once belonged to Cardinal Fabbroni. Gori's philosophy for his ongoing collection is based on two underly-

ing principles: one, that talented artists should have a place in which they are free to create and two, that the indivisible relationship between art and nature must always be respected. At this writing, more than seventy works are on display, mostly outdoors.

Pistoletto, Paladino, Spoldi, Vedova, and Nicola de Maria represent the Italian school; Sol Le Witt from the U.S., Richard Long from Britain, as well as Alice Aycock, Dennis Oppenheim, and Anne and Patrick Poirier are among the most prominent non-Italian artists.

Pistoia has produced major architectural monuments in every period of Italian art. Some outstanding examples are, in chronological order, the Romanesque Duomo, the Gothic Baptistery, the Renaissance Ospedale del Ceppo, and the Baroque church of Spirito Santo. People come to Pistoia to breathe the pure mountain air of the nearby mountains, recreate their childhood memories of Pinocchio at Collodi, and taste the exquisite local specialties such as confetti, brigidini, and necci.

PISTOIA

Pistoia has something for everyone: art, horticulture, spas, and food specialties from the mountains and the valleys. Settled by the Romans, it was where the Roman conspirator Catiline died in 62 B.C. During the Middle Ages, it thrived as a free commune, until it was annexed to Florence in the 16th century. Today, Pistoia is the capital of a varied region renowned for its forest-covered mountains, that are popular both as summer and winter resorts, and its verdant Valdinievole Valley, which vaunts one of Italy's major horticulture centers, Pescia. Gastronomically speaking, Pistoia is famous for simple country and mountain dishes. The haute cuisine of nearby Montecatini, the internationally renowned spa, draws gourmets from all over the world.

Romanesque facade of the Duomo (right), and belltower (far right).

The historic center of Pistoia is Piazza del Duomo, with its medieval architectural masterpieces: the **Duomo**, characterized by a Romanesque facade adorned with three rows of blind arcading, the elegant Tuscan Gothic **Baptistery**, designed by Andrea Pisano and Cellino di Nese in the 14th century; **Palazzo del Comune**, a Gothic masterpiece designed at the turn of the 13th century; and **Palazzo Pretorio**, a Gothic building adorned with two-part windows and coats-of-arms.

Two Romanesque churches, **San Giovanni Fuorcivitas**, with its Tuscan Romanesque striped facade, and **Sant'Andrea**, contain especially important works. In the former is the *pulpit* by **Fra Guglielmo di Pisa** (1270); in the latter is the *pulpit* by **Giovanni Pisano** (1298-1301).

The grandiose **church of Santo Spirito** (1647) near the Duomo is a fine example of Roman-style Baroque. The interior, adorned with elaborate marble decorations, contains an *altar* attributed to **Bernini**, a splendid Flemish organ, and a huge *altarpiece* by **Pietro da Cortona**.

Inside the 12th century **church of San Bartolomeo in Pantano** is a Romanesque *pulpit* carved by **Guido da Como**.

The 13th century **Ospedale del Ceppo** (Hospital of the Hollow Treetrunk), which is still functioning as a health care center today, was named after its "collection box" made out of a hollowed-out treetrunk. Above its elegant porch is the monument that is perhaps most closely related to the city's history: the glazed

And, for dessert, confetti *and* confortini

Confetti *(sugar-coated almond candies) are eaten every day in Pistoia and not, as happens elsewhere, only on special occasions such as weddings. Mentioned in documents dating from the 14th and 15th centuries, they were originally distributed on the feast day of the city's patron, St. James of Campostela. Round and white, they look and taste different from the* confetti *produced in other Italian regions—and indeed the traditional recipe is a well-kept secret. Don't forget to pick up a bag of Pistoia* confetti *made from "the finest sugar and almonds" before you leave.* Confortini *(literally, tiny comforters) are little cakes made of sugar and syrup, which, once upon a time, street vendors used to sell at fairs and festas. Their name comes from the comfort reputedly given by the taste of the liquor.*

Masterpiece musts

The Gothic *pulpit* by **Giovanni Pisano** in the Romanesque *church of Sant'Andrea* is universally acclaimed as one of the finest medieval sculpted pulpits extant in Pistoia or anywhere. Supported by

seven columns with sculpted capitals, it is elaborately carved with scenes in high and low relief. In the Duomo, you can admire one of Italy's great silversmithing masterpieces, the *St. Jacob Altar,* crafted between the 13th and 15th centuries, and the *tomb of Cardinal Forteguerri,* designed by Early Renaissance master, **Verrocchio**, in 1473.

Above: *Della Robbia frieze on the* **Ospedale del Ceppo.**

Pistoia specialties

When dining in Pistoia, we recommend the simple, historic dishes that constitute the local specialties. Don't be afraid of asking the waiter for *"il carcerato"* (the prisoner) made of beef giblets, seasoned with pepper, butter, and aged *pecorino* cheese, which long ago was the prisoners' fare in the City of Pistoia jails. To freshen your palate, order a hearty bowl of *briachina* (literally, the tipsy one), a salad green with wine-colored (hence, tipsy) striations grown in nearby Pescia, which has become a favorite of modern-day salad-mavens *Bertoli*, a simple, delicious treat, are sun-dried apple sections "imported" from the nearby mountains.

Above: church of San Giovanni Fuorcivitas, 12th-13th centuries. Below: medieval marketplace, Piazza della Sala.

terracotta *frieze*, a 16th century work by the Della Robbia school, depicting the Seven Acts of Mercy (e.g., visiting the sick and imprisoned, clothing the naked, giving lodging to pilgrims)—proof that the *Pistoiesi* regarded history not only in terms of war and battles, but also in terms of solidarity and charity (providing shelter and food for the needy).

Piazza della Sala: the thousand-year-old marketplace

If you want the experience of doing the marketing the way the Pistoiesi *have been doing it since the Middle Ages, head for* Piazza della Sala *(whose name in Longobard means "royal palace"), which has been the city's most popular meeting and market place for the last one thousand years. Of artistic note are the building facades and the monumental* well *in the center, which was designed by Cecchino di Giaggio in 1453. (The Marzocco lion, the symbol of Florence, on top is a later addition.) Of gastronomic note is the fresh produce sold in the historic roofed stalls.*

MONTECATINI: THE TOWN AND SPA

For over eight centuries renowned for its mineral springs and for over two centuries one of Europe's most fashionable spas, Montecatini today attracts upwards of two million visitors a year, who not only come to restore their health, but also to socialize in the town's elegant 18th-century-style hotels and bathing establishments. Aside from "taking the waters" in one of the nine thermal spas open to the public, visitors can enjoy open-air concerts, horse-racing at the Ippodromo Sesana, golfing, or just strolling in the city's 420,000 square meters of parks and gardens. Two of the oldest spas, the **Tettuccio** and the **Terme Leopoldine**, are among the most popular. Montecatini owes its fame to the 14th century physician, Ugolino Simoni, founder of the Italian school of hydrology and author of the famous tome *De Balneorum Italiae Proprietatibus*, who first described the mineral water's health benefits, especially for the liver. Among the famous names associated with Montecatini are Grandduke Pietro Leopoldo, who, in the late 1700s, commissioned the still-operating Terme Leopoldine, as well as composers Giuseppe Verdi, who wrote parts of *Otello* and *Falstaff* in the spa he visited for twenty seasons starting in 1882, and Giacomo Puccini, who was also a faithful visitor.

World-class cuisine

While the restaurants in the Valdinievole Valley and the nearby mountain area serve plain country cooking, Montecatini is renowned for its world-class cuisine—and for the hotel management school which turns out the superbly trained chefs who prepare it. Smart tourists can get the best of both worlds by alternating ultra-refined French dishes with hearty country fare. The local specialties are *cialde* (cakes) made of flour, milk, eggs, and almonds and the produce of the Valdinievole Valley. There is also a fine white wine, *Bianco della Valdinievole*, which was awarded Doc (controlled origin) certification in 1976.

Above: Terme del Tettuccio *spa.* *Entrance to the* Excelsior spa (**far left**) *and Montecatini* Alta (**left**).

Cioncia and *Sorana Beans*

Among the Valdinievole Valley specialties, which are a unique mix of the very plain and the very elaborate, are *farro* soups, fried frogs, and *berlingozzo*, a seasonal cake. But the most famous of all are the *Sorana beans*, which are ultrarare (no more than five thousand kilos are produced in a season) and ultradelicous (skinless and amazingly tender). The celebrated 19th century Italian author, Edmondo De Amicis, wrote that *Sorana beans* are appreciated in places as far away as Costantinopolis and that they should only be exported to other European nations as if they were jewels.

Giant asparagus is another great veggie grown in the region—it tastes even better after having been dipped in local olive oil. *Cioncia* is a meat specialty of Pescia whose origin is unknown, although it is most likely connected with the tanning of hides, which is still a major occupation in the region. The dish is made of flesh scraped from the heads, tails, and faces of slaughtered cows. The flesh is washed, boiled, and then sautéed in onions and basil with wine and chili pepper added for flavor. It must be cooked for several hours to make it edible.

Above: *view of Valdinievole from Massa e Cozzile. Pescia: Porta Fiorentina* (right) *and Duomo* (far right).

PESCIA and the verdant dream of the VALDINIEVOLE

Pescia, the city of flowers, was founded in the 11th century and was thereafter the object of a centuries-long tug-of-war between Lucca and Florence. Entering by way of the old city gate, **Porta Fiorentina**, you soon reach the splendid **Cathedral** with some notable historic buildings along the way. Don't miss the **church of San Francesco** which contains *frescoes* by **Lorenzo Bicci** and the *St. Francis Altarpiece* painted by **Bonaventura Berlinghieri** in the 13th century. Nearby is **Monsummano**, a thriving industrial center (shoe manufacture) and famed for its natural-steam **spa**. Health-seekers will enjoy a bath in the 30°C waters of the celebrated **Grotta Giusti** and the **Grotta Parlanti**.

With over 1500 wholesale florists growing flowers on over 3000 hectares and almost two million square meters of greenhouses, Pescia is one of Italy's two major flower exporters (the other is Sanremo in Liguria) and its biggest grower of carnations. It hosts two important trade shows, the International Flower Market and the Flower Biennial. Undeniably, the Valdinievole Valley represents a unique Tuscan combination of great flowers and great food.

Lamporecchio, one of the Valdinievole Valley's feudal strongholds, is renowned for a pastry specialty, *brigidini* (page 84), and an architectural masterpiece by **Bernini**, **Villa Rospigliosi di Spicchio**. Several other villas between Monsummano and Lamporecchio are worthy of a detour, especially **Villa Medicea** at Montevettolini, **Villa Poggi-Banchieri** at Castelmartini, and **Villa Forini-Lippi** and **Villa L'Oliveta** near Montecatini. Of special note are **Villa Bellavista** at Borgo a Buggiano, a fine example of the 17th century Tuscan Baroque style, the 17th century **Villa Garzoni** at Collodi (which is described on the next page), and the 18th century **Villa Sermolli**.

Above: *flower market in Pescia.*

AGRITURISMO – *A restful country vacation amidst olive groves and vineyards in the homeland of Leonardo da Vinci and the Medici family*

The scenic countryside of olive groves and vineyards around Pescia, Montecatini, and Lamporecchio make the area popular for agriturismo. *Whether you prefer relaxing in a comfortable villa or a renovated castle, or whether you prefer a more rustic farmhouse vacation that includes putting time in the vineyard, olive grove, vegetable garden, or orchard, there's something for you.*

There are also many nearby sights to explore, foremost of which are the Museo della Ceramica in Montelupo Fiorentino, Leonardo's birthplace and the Leonardo Museum in Vinci, and the Medici Villa in Artimino.

Collodi, Pinocchioland

Above: monument to
Pinocchio, *Collodi*
(left), Villa Garzoni
garden, *Collodi*
(center),
and Grotta Giusti,
Monsummano
(right).

Pinocchio, the most celebrated character in children's literature, was created in 1881 by Tuscan journalist, Carlo Lorenzini, who took his pen name, Carlo Collodi, from the name of his birthplace. The world of Pinocchio, from the Red Shrimp Inn to the Land of Toys, has been recreated by celebrated modern artists, including Emilio Greco, Venturino Venturi, and Pietro Consagra in Collodi's unique version of Disneyland.

Nearby is a treat for grownups, **Villa Garzoni**, an outstanding example of Tuscan Mannerism, which is set amidst a lovely formal garden.

Brigidini *of Lamporecchio: sweet balls of fire*

Artusi, the renowned 19th century Italian chef, dubbed brigidini *"that special Tuscan treat." First mentioned in 17th century documents preserved in Lamporecchio, their name probably comes from Santa Brigida, the location of the convent belonging to the cloistered nuns who supposedly created them (nuns being renowned all over Italy for their pastry expertise!). No longer confined to convents,* brigidini *are served piping hot at fairs and festas all over Tuscany.*

Today, Lamporecchio has over one hundred brigidini *pastry shops, where the fragrant little balls of flour, eggs, sugar, and anise flavoring are cooked in electric ovens—and no longer in the traditional "ferri da cialde" (cookie irons). Stop off at Lamporecchio for a taste (although, since they smell and taste so good, don't expect to eat just one) on your way to the splendid Villa Rospigliosi, which* **Bernini** *designed in 1669.*

Necci: bread or brioche?

It is hardly surprising that chestnuts, king of the Pistoia Mountains, are the main ingredient of *necci*, the region's specialty. Locals eat the little round cakes of unleavened chestnut flour with a dash of salt just as they would bread—with everything. Visitors, instead, like to roll them, stuffed with *ricotta* cheese, into sandwiches. Like *brigidini*, *necci* are no longer baked in the traditional way, placed between two stone disks in a wood-burning oven.

The recipe varies according to whether you eat them in one of the mountain villages, in the Garfagnana or Lunigiana regions, or in the towns of Massa (where they are called *"bollenti"* literally, hot cakes) or Carrara.

The Pistoia Mountains: Tuscany's year-round natureland

The Pistoia Mountains, with miles of uncontaminated forests and waterways, are tourist attractions all year round. Among the popular resort towns are **San Marcello Pistoiese**, settled by the Romans, which is set amid fir and chestnut forests, **Cutigliano**, **Maresca**, and **Gavinana**. Don't miss the **Ponte Sospeso di Mammiano** on the Lima River near San Marcello Pistoiese. **Abetone**, situated 1400 meters above sea level at the pass, is a skier's paradise in winter and a hiker's paradise in summer. The town is the creation of Grandduke Pietro Leopoldo, who built the access road and dedicated the two pyramids indicating the borderline between the territories of Tuscany and Modena in 1778.

Above: *ski slopes, Abetone.*
Left: *tour map of the Montagna Pistoiese and Palazzo Pretorio, Cutigliano (insert).*

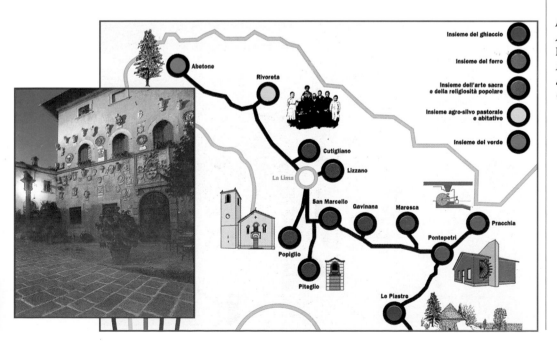

Insieme del ghiaccio
Insieme del ferro
Insieme dell'arte sacra e della religiosità popolare
Insieme agro-silvo pastorale e abitativo
Insieme del verde

Abetone
Rivoreta
Cutigliano
Lizzano
La Lima
San Marcello
Gavinana
Maresca
Pracchia
Pontepetri
Popiglio
Piteglio
Le Piastre

THE CHESTNUT REPORT

How green are our chestnuts

Tuscany, one of Italy's most wooded regions, is in large part covered with chestnut forests. This is hardly surprising because since Roman times its plains have been cultivated with cereals and its mountains with chestnut trees. For this reason, the delicate green of the chestnut groves dominates much of the landscape of the Pistoiese Apennines, as well as the Amiata, Garfagnana, Lunigiana, and Casentino districts. (Fir trees, which rank second, give the medieval forests of Camaldoli and Vallombrosa a more intense hue.)

It's hard to get at the chestnuts, which have to be gathered from the ground and then extracted from their spiny protective shells, but, once you do, it's easy to make them into delicious foods. In the words of an anonymous historian: "as the silent friend of the poorer people in a land of abundant mountains and forests, the chestnut is a welcome and trustworthy presence."

The nutritional value of chestnuts

The chart on the right reveals that the nutritional value of chestnuts, especially when they are boiled, is comparable to that of bread. This explains how up to the 20th century the peasants in the poorer areas survived during the years of famine exclusively on a diet based on *polenta* made of ground chestnuts and bread made of chestnut flour.

per 100 grams	chestnuts	boiled chestnuts	bread (00 flour)
calories	181	297	279
protein	1,8	4,7	8,7
sugar	39,4	67	64,7
fat	2,9	3	0,2

Chestnuts coming up!

Every part of the chestnut is consumed; not a single bit is wasted or discarded. If they're eaten boiled, they're called *"ballotte"* (little balls), whereas roasted, they're called *"bruciate"* ("burned ones"). *Dried chestnuts* can be eaten raw or cooked. Last but not least, chestnuts can be ground into a flour, known *"farina dolce"* (sweet flour), for which dozens of recipes exist. One of the best known is *"castagnaccio"*, a chestnut cake popular all over Tuscany. Chestnut flour is also used to make the Tuscan version of polenta which is known as *"pattona."* *"Fritelle di farina dolce"* (chestnut pancakes) and *necci*, which are often eaten, rolled up and stuffed with a soft cheese such as ricotta, are still favorites in the Pistoia area. Although chestnuts are traditionally classified as a peasant food, oddly enough, desserts made with chestnuts are considered worthy of the most aristocratic tables. Among the best known are *Monte Bianco* (an elaborate dessert made of chestnuts, milk, vanilla, sugar, and whipped cream), *budino di marroni* (chestnut pudding), *castagne sciroppate* (chestnuts with syrup), and *gelato di marroni* (chestnut ice cream). And what better elite treat than *marrons glacés* (sugar-glazed boiled chestnuts)...

When you're traveling around Tuscany in winter, look out for the street vendors selling "bruciate", and buy a bag hot off the coals. In the best, most genuine Tuscan trattorie*, a favorite dessert is a slice of* castagnaccio*, washed down with a nice glass of "vino rosso novello" (young red wine).* Castagnaccio *is so easy to make, we've included a recipe below.*

Recipe for castagnaccio
(traditional Tuscan chestnut cake)

Ingredients: 1/2 kilo of chestnut flour, 100 grams of pinenuts, a handful of raisins, four tablespoons of olive oil, a dash of salt, a sprig of rosemary.
1. Mix the chestnut flour and water, while adding the oil, pinenuts, raisins, and salt.
2. When the dough is smooth, pour in a well greased pan. The level should not exceed that of one finger.
3. Scatter some rosemary and oil on top.
4. Bake in preheated hot oven around 45 minutes or until a deeply cracked crust forms.

"Poorman's delicacy"

When Tuscans hear the word *"montagna"* (mountain), they tend to associate it with chestnuts which, from the Middle Ages, have been regarded as the food of the poor. Today, chest-

nuts have taken on a symbolic, almost sacred meaning: they have become food to be enjoyed in dozens of different ways, accompanied by a delicate *vino novello.* Folklore has it that, while chestnuts may cause heartburn and swelling, their chief function is to purify body and soul.

Chestnuts appear as ingredients in a host of popular recipes such as *"minestra di penitenza"* (repentance soup). Mixed with wheat flour, they are often used to make bread. Not only are raw or cooked chestnut dishes nutritious, they also are used in helping to treat certain illnesses such as respiratory diseases. It is no wonder that for centuries chestnuts, like acorns, regarded as being fit only for animals and the poor, have been known as "the poorman's delicacy."

Originally settled by the Romans, Lucca was the capital of the Longobard reign of Tuscia during the early medieval period. It thrived during the later Middle Ages as a commune and—except for brief periods of subjugation under the adventurer, Castruccio Castracani, and a local lord, Paolo Guinigi—as a free republic from the 14th century onward. Thereafter, it prospered on trade and agriculture. In the 19th century, it was ruled as an independent grandduchy by Napoleon's sister, Elisa Baciocchi, and then as a duchy by Maria Luisa di Borbone. During the 1800s, a major urban renewal campaign was carried out, during which time the city walls (whose third, and final, circle dates from the 16th century republic) were turned into a public park, and the two great squares, Piazza Napoleone and Piazza del Mercato, were built. In 1847, Lucca was annexed to the Grandduchy of Tuscany—yet it has never lost its proud autonomy and its unique appearance of an eminent capital city.

Not just an art center, Lucca is a shopper's paradise, renowned for the sober elegance of its shops. For centuries, it has been famous for its textile and paper industries and for a most unusual craft—that of making plaster statuettes—which *Lucchesi* emigrants have carried with them throughout the world. Its culinary specialties include *farro* grain, fine wines, and one of Italy's best olive oils.

Although there are dozens of sights to enjoy in the "city of the hundred churches," as Lucca has been called, three—the Duomo, Piazza del Mercato, and the city walls encircling the historic center—are absolute musts. You can't say you've seen Lucca unless you visit them!

The first of the three musts, the **Duomo**, dedicated to St. Martin, was started as a Romanesque building, but it was completed centuries later in the Tuscan Gothic style. On the left side of the portico are sculpted scenes of the *Nativity* (along the architrave) and the *Deposition* (in the lunette) ascribed to **Nicola Pisano**. The interior contains important

Above: city walls, *Lucca.*
Below: tomb of Ilaria del Carretto *by Jacopo della Quercia,* Duomo *(1408).*

The township of Lucca covers a vast and varied territory extending over the Alpi Apuane mountains, the Garfagnana plains, and the Versilia coast. Its art spans the centuries, from 11th century castles, medieval city states, and Renaissance towns to Art Nouveau in Viareggio and contemporary sculpture in Pietrasanta. It is also renowned for its excellent cuisine, based on fresh vegetables and grains, and for its topnotch olive oil.

works such as **Tintoretto's** *Last Supper,* an *altarpiece* by **Ghirlandaio**, and the octagonal *Tempietto* built to protect a medieval *Crucifix* and the *Holy Face*, perhaps an Oriental work, mentioned by Dante in the *Divine Comedy*. However, to most people, the most remarkable work in the Duomo is the *tomb of Ilaria del Carretto*, carved by **Jacopo della Quercia** in 1408, which immortalizes the exquisite young wife of Paolo Guinigi, Lord of Lucca, in the eternal sleep of premature death.

The second of the three musts, the majestic **city walls**, are the best preserved of their kind in Italy. The walls are four kilometers in girth and twelve feet tall, interspersed with eleven scenic bastions and a moat, which has been splendidly landscaped. Built as defense walls

between the 16th and 17th centuries, they never, however, were subjected to enemy attack. They were turned into a public park by Grandduchess Elisa Baciocchi at the turn of the 19th century.

The last of the three musts, the **Piazza del Mercato**, rises over the old Roman amphitheater, which explains its unusual elliptical shape. Completely surrounded by residential buildings whose tenants are called *"piazzaioli"* (piazza dwellers), it has only four entranceways. The piazza is the masterpiece of town-planner **Lorenzo Nottolini**, who was one of the architects responsible for the great urban renewal project carried out in the 19th century. On holidays, to the delight of the populace, the elliptical space was used for open-air bingo games.

Above: Canova Painting a Portrait of Elisa Baciocchi *by P. Benvenuti.* Below: Torre Guinigi, *with its "rooftop garden" of holmoak trees.*

Shopping and dropping on Via Fillungo

Emerging from Piazza dell'Anfiteatro, you find yourself on Via Fillungo, one of Italy's most renowned shopping streets, which slices right through Lucca's historic center. It is lined on both sides with medieval towerhouses whose ground floors have been turned into refined shops with gorgeous displays of everything from fabrics to foods, making it the city's elegant shopping street—and also its busiest. On Via Fillungo, you shop till you drop...into one of the many delightful coffeehouses along it, for example, the historic Caffè Caselli. (See "The Coffee Report.")

Pontormo captures a Medici

Two fine arts museums are well worth a visit: the *National Painting Gallery* (since 1819) in the 17th century *Palazzo Mansi* and the *Museo Nazionale di Villa Guinigi*, located just outside the city walls. The highlights of the former are the celebrated *Camera degli Sposi* (Marriage Chamber), the *portrait of Alessandro dei Medici* painted by the Mannerist master Pontormo in 1525, as well as works by Bronzino, Tintoretto, Veronese Luca Giordano and Dolci. The highlights of the latter are sculpture by Matteo Civitali and Baccio da Montelupo, *crucifixes* by Berlinghiero Berlinghieri and Orlandi, as well as masterpieces of the minor arts and church fittings.

Top: *Piazza del Mercato renovated in the 19th century by Lorenzo Nottolini.*

Before making the grand tour of churches, stop to admire Lucca's wonderful buildings and palaces, including the **Palazzo Pretorio** designed by native son **Matteo Civitali**, the **medieval houses of Chiasso Barletti**, the **Palazzo della Provincia** by **Ammannati**, the **Palazzi Guinigi**, and the lovely **Casa Pfanner** on Via degli Asili.

One of the most important churches is **San Michele in Foro**, built between the 12th and 14th centuries. Its facade with four rows of arcading is a striking example of the Pisan-Lucchese Romanesque style. Inside are works by **Andrea della Robbia** and **Filippino Lippi**.

Above: portrait of Alessandro de' Medici *by Pontormo,* Pinacoteca (left), Duomo (center), *and* San Michele in Foro (right).

200 years of aroma

The real Tuscan

Of the four types of Tuscan cigars, all of which are produced by the government owned Monopolio di Stato, only one is regarded as the genuine "old Tuscan smoke" and only one is entirely made by hand: the aromatic "toscano" manufactured by Lucca's Manifattura Tabacchi (and in the United States and Argentina under Italian license).

The fragrance of a toscano *is highly valued as a stimulant for digestion and conversation. Containing five grams of pure Kentucky tobacco aged for two years, it originated through a serendipitous fluke at the turn of the 19th century, when a bale of tobacco was soaked in a rainstorm. The nimble-fingered "sigaraie" (cigar ladies) of Lucca turn out up to 600* toscani *a day!*

Another is **San Frediano**, built between the 12th and 13th centuries, whose plain facade is adorned with a huge mosaic of the *Ascension of Christ* executed by followers of **Berlinghiero Berlinghieri**. Inside are **Della Robbia** glazed *terracottas*, a Romanesque *font*, and two *sculpted tombs* by **Jacopo della Quercia**.

Above: facade *of* San Frediano *decorated with a mosaic of the Ascension of Christ.*

Buccellato: Lucca's Cake of Good Horn

The first mention of Lucca's favorite cake, *buccellato*, dates back to a 15th century document. Presumably, it was named after the *buccina*, the Roman trumpet, whose shape it resembles. The traditional ingredients—

once, but no longer, secret—are water, flour, yeast, sugar, anise, and raisins. Some recipes call for eggs and butter. Served hot, in thin slices, it is best accompanied by a glass of one of the delicious red or white local wines. Biting into a piece of *buccellato* wasn't always the carefree gesture it is today, since the tempting cake was once a favorite with poisoners!

VILLE LUCCHESI

LORDS OF THE HILLS

Built between the 16th and 18th centuries, the great villas dotting the environs of Lucca *(ville lucchesi)* are an extraordinary lot. Many are scenically situated in the surrounding hills, not far from waterways (to facilitate the watering of gardens). Adorned with porches and arcades in an unusual combination of the Doric and Tuscan orders, they sport polychrome plaster-on-stone facades. The 17th century **Villa Mansi di Segromigno** (left) has a striking facade. Once surrounded by a splendid formal garden designed by a group of landscape architects that included Juvara, it now has a wilder, more romantic setting. **Villa Torrigiani** (right), also built in the 17th century in an imposing Mannerist style, has a remarkable interior of frescoed rooms and a French garden setting. Lastly, the simple and harmonious **Villa Reale di Marlia**, vaunts a splendid garden with a theater.

Above: Villa Mansi *at Segromigno* (left) *and* Villa Torrigiani *at Camigliano* (right).

Center: library *belonging to author Francesca Duanti in a villa outside Lucca.* Right: *typical plaster figurines made in Lucca.*

Plaster craft

Many of those who left the Garfagnana in the 1800s to seek their fortune in North America made their living selling plaster statuettes. Today, the last of the figurinai, *as these simple craftsmen are called, work in the three factories still operating in the town of Coreglia Antelminelli, near Barga. You can learn more about them in the Plaster Crafts and Emigration Museum.*

THE GARFAGNANA:
history, nature, and good cooking

Situated in the upper reaches of the Serchio Valley which stretches across the Apuan and Apennine mountains, the **Garfagnana** region is renowned for its scenic beauty. A good place to start sightseeing is the historic town of **Castelnuovo**, whose major sights include a Renaissance **Duomo**, with *Della Robbia terracottas* and a 15th century wood *crucifix*, and the **Ponte Castruccio** bridge. Nearby is the **Convento dei Cappuccini**, the monastery where the poet and district governor, **Ludovico Ariosto**, resided under Alfonso III d'Este. The popular resort town of **Castiglione di Garfagnana**, vaunts a scenic setting and two fine churches, **San Michele** and **San Pietro**.

On the way back to Lucca, stop at **Barga**. The upper section of the town is of Longobard origin, while the lower part stretching along the plain is modern. The most important sight is the stupendous 9th century Romanesque **Duomo**, with a plain travertine facade adorned only by a carved portal, and a flanking crenelated **belltower**. Inside is a 13th centu-

Farro: renaissance of a grain

Farro (spelt), the staple grain of Ancient Rome, was gradually supplanted by wheat and corn until it virtually disappeared—except in the Garfagnana and Lunigiana regions. Today, having made a glorious comeback as a gourmet specialty, it is served in many of Italy's finest restaurants. As nutritious as it is delicious, it is used in everything from soup to dessert, from *"minestra di farro"* (farro soup, which, in addition to *farro*, often contains pasta and beans) to *"torta di farro"* (farro pie). A local specialty combines *farro e riso* (farro and rice): The two grains are cooked separately and then mixed with cheese, salt and pepper, nutmeg, and lemon peel.

Above: *Tereglio in Garfagnana.*
Center: Duomo, *Barga.*
Below: Ponte del Diavolo, *Borgo a Mozzano.*

ry marble *pulpit* and an 11th century carved wooden *statue of St. Christopher*. Other sights include the delightful **Palazzo Pretorio** adorned a 14th century arcade, the **Logget-ta del Podestà**, the **Palazzo Comunale**, and the **Loggia del Mercato**. Outside the city gates is the **church-monastery of San Francesco**, with the *Altarpiece of the Assumption* attributed to **Giovanni Della Rob-**

bia. Nearby is **Castelvecchio Pascoli**, named after **Giovanni Pascoli**, who dedicated the verses of *Canti di Castelvecchio* to the town. You can visit the home and grave of the great Italian poet, who lived here from 1895 to 1912.

Four of the Garfagnana's most interesting and unusual museums are located in the same general area. This makes it easy to visit them

The Calomini Hermitage

Stunningly perched on a 345-meter-high rock wall in the Tùrrite di Gallicano Valley, the *Calomini Hermitage* was originally erected in the 7th century by the hermits populating the nearby grottoes and later rebuilt in the 17th century. The sanctuary is a later addition. The present-day structure, dedicated to the Virgin, has been recently restored. Guests receive a place to meditate, lodging, and delicious food.

Above: hermitage of Calomini (small photo), *the gorge called* "Orrido di Botri" (center), *and Vagli di Sotto whose waters conceal a 13th century town* (right).

Greens in Garfagnana: not just salad

Although Tuscans are known to be big steak eaters, they are exceedingly fond of their vegetables as well—especially those grown in the Garfagnana region, which are highly prized for their flavor and freshness.

One of the most popular regional specialties is a soup made of corn, beans, cabbage, oil, and grated parmesan or pecorino *cheese, which is called* incatenata *(chained),* incavolata *(angry),* intruglia *(potion), depending on where you order it: Exquisite are the wild greens with lilting*

names such as pimpirinella, dolcetta, va-lerianella, salvastrella, cicerbita, borrana, *and* tarassaco, *which can be eaten separately, raw or boiled or added to soups and omelets as flavor-enhancers.*

Fortresses and castles

The environs of Lucca, especially the upper Serchio Valley, abound with feudal fortresses built between the 11th and 13th century, and castles, built in later centuries, surrounded by the traditional protective walls and moats. Erected to defend towns which, under the rule of Borso d'Este, were termed "new lands," the fortresses have survived in surprisingly good condition, those of Verrucole, Monte Alfonso, Castiglione, and Castelnuovo, being virtually intact. Many of the castles have also survived. There are over twenty waiting to be discovered along the way.

Above: *one of the many Garfagnana castles.*
Below: casino, *Bagni di Lucca.*

all, starting from the **Museum of Rural Life** ("The Farm Labor Report") at **San Pellegrino in Alpe**, then the **Museum of Plaster Crafts and Emigration** (sidebar) at **Coreglia Antelminelli**, followed by the **Chestnut Museum** at **Colognora**, and finally the **Arts and Crafts Museum**, (exhibiting mainly laces) at **Castelnuovo**.

Curiosities. Among the curiosities to be found in the Garfagnana, perhaps the best known is the asymmetric **Ponte del Diavolo** (Devil's Bridge) at **Borgo a Mozzano** near Barga. Not far away, in a scenic setting, is the **Grotta del Vento**, a grotto much used in scientific studies, which runs for a kilometer between waterfalls and fossil-filled caves. Nearby, at Tereglio, is the so-called "**Orrido di Botri**" (Botri horror), a breathtaking natural crevice between two mountains. A whole 13th century town, **Fabbriche**, lies beneath the waters of the **lake-basin of Vagli di Sotto**, which has been closed off by a dam to produce electricity. Normally, only the bell-tower emerges from the water, but the whole town surfaces every ten years when the basin is emptied for maintenance.

Bagni di Lucca, the 2000-year-old spa

Once upon a time, Bagni di Lucca, situated in the Lima River Valley, was a fashionable spa and resort town. Its nineteen springs of calcium- and sulfate-rich mineral water have been known since Antiquity. In 1284, Guidone da Corvaia cited the health benefits of bathing in its waters in his *Cronaca Pisana*. **Montaigne** was a visitor in the 16th century.

However, the town only reached its apex of fame in the 1800s when Carlo Ludovico di Borbone, whose royal palace was in Lucca, made it a watering place for the intellectuals and jet set of the day. Among its famed visitors were **Byron**, **Shelley**, **Heine**, and **Carducci**. Its pleasant climate, scenic setting, and

fascinating monuments warrant a stopover. The major sights are the oldest spa called **Bagno Caldo** or **Bagno di Corsena**, the **Casino Municipale** (1840), the **Demidoff Hospital** and **Chapel** (1827), and the **Anglican Church** and **Cemetery** (1839).

Tuscan gold

In excess of 20 million liters of olive oil are produced annually in Tuscany, from the hills flanking the Versilia coast to the Casentino Valley, from Siena to Arezzo to Florence.
Nothing beats an old fashioned oil mill.

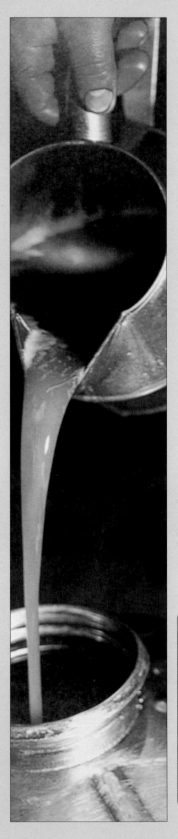

Every year Tuscany's 43,000 *olivicoltori* produce in excess of 20 million liters of olive oil, mostly of the extra virgin variety. Olive groves are to be found throughout in the region—you can ideally follow them from the Versilia hills near the coast, past the Casentino mountains and the hills flanking the Greve and Pesa Rivers, through the districts of Arezzo, Siena, and finally to Florence. Proportionally, 8% of Tuscan olive oil is made from olives grown in plains and 10% is made from olives grown in mountain areas, while a whooping 82%, is made from olives grown in hilly areas. Unfortunately, about every fifty years, an especially severe cold spell hits Tuscany that kills the olive trees. The most recent one, in 1985, destroyed half of the trees.

Tuscan olives, of the *frantoio*, *leccino*, *maurino*, and *puntino* varieties, are the first to be harvested in Italy. Individually hand-picked, the ripe olives are collected in enormous cloths laid at the

From Noah to Picasso: the olive as a symbol

The olive spread, possibly from the Caucasus, throughout the Mediterranean basin. By 4000 B.C. there were olive trees in Palestine. By 2500 B.C., the rules regarding the trade and commerce of olive oil had been set down in a Babylonian edict.

To the ancient peoples, the olive was regarded as sacred. In ancient Greece, anyone who damaged an olive was put on trial; Homer sang its praises in the Odyssey. *In the*

foot of the trees called *paracadute* (parachutes) and then taken to the mill for processing. (Exhibits in the Museum of Rural Life describe the oil-making process and equipment.) In some Tuscan mills, there are still traditional stone olive-grinding wheels, although in most places they have been supplanted by modern high-powered steel presses.

Italy, one of the world's largest producers of olive oil along with Spain and Greece, has steadily increased exports to meet the growing demand as more and more people worldwide convert to the Mediterranean diet. A case in point is the United States, which in few years has quintupled annual importation from 20,000 to 100,000 tons per year. Even Japan, traditionally a consumer of soy and colzaseed oil, is now one of the world's biggest importers of olive oil.

Old Testament, *the announcement to Noah that the Flood was over was made by a dove carrying an olive branch. In the* New Testament, *Jesus is called the "Christ" which means "the one anointed with oil."* (kristòs *in Greek). The Agony of Garden took place on the Mount of Olives. In the* Koran, *the holy book of Islam, the olive is called "the blessed tree."*

In every Mediterranean culture, the olive symbolizes fertility and peace. The Catholic priest uses olive oil to anoint those receiving the sacrament of confirmation and those receiving last rites. One of the most significant works by the greatest painter of our times, Picasso, is a drawing of a dove with an olive branch. Amazingly, two Tuscan olive trees have been alive for thousands of years. One known as "Olivo della Strega" (witch's olive tree) is in Magliano near Grosseto, the other known as "l'Olivone" (big olive tree) is in Saturnia.

The Mediterranean diet awash in a sea of olive oil

Use it raw as a condiment, fry in it, sauté with it. It's the main ingredient of pinzimonio *and* fettunta, *two of Tuscany's favorite foods.*

Olive oil sommeliers

The term *"olive oil sommelier"* originated in 1984, the year the *Corporazione dei Mastri Oleari* (Guild of the Olive Oil Professionals) was established. Like wine sommeliers, olive oil sommeliers must be able to analyze every aspect of the product. Before tasting it, they must first visually inspect it (is it smooth, clear, cloudy?), smell it (how fruity is it?) and touch it (how viscous, oily is it?). Training courses for prospective olive oil sommeliers are held in Bettolle (near Siena), Montevarchi (near Arezzo), and in Florence. To obtain certification, you must have experience in olive-growing, be knowledgeable about the oil-making processes, and possess a well-trained set of tastebuds. Olive oil consortiums, such as the Consorzio delle Terre del Gallo Nero, the Laudemio Consorzio, and the Consorzio della Provincia di Siena, have also been established to further protect and promote the quality of Tuscan extra virgin olive oils.

Unlike Northern Italy which dotes on butter and rice, Southern and Central Italy favor olive oil and pasta. In Tuscany, cooking without olive oil would be unthinkable, if not impossible. It is used raw as a condiment, especially in salad dressings. It is used to fry in and sauté with. With a little salt and vinegar, it is served with the Tuscan version of crudités known as *pinzimonio*. It is the main ingredient of the glorious country specialty *"fettunta"*

Olive oil: for light, beauty, and health

Olive oil was not always regarded as a food. Throughout Antiquity, people used it to smooth and moisturize their skin after bathing; athletes, especially runners and wrestlers, would rub it over their bodies to warm up their muscles. Before becoming popular as food, olive oil was

(oily slice), which is simply a thick slice of toasted country-style Tuscan bread lightly coated with garlic and sometimes with sliced tomato, over which olive oil has been lavished.

Tuscan olive oil has a limpid, translucent appearance, except when it's *nuovo* (new, or just milled). New oil, by contrast, is drab olive green and far less limpid. It has a distinctive tangy taste—the younger the oil, the stronger its tang—and a fruity smell, which varies according to where the olives were grown.

Today, dietitians recommend frying in olive oil, rather than seed oil, because of the health benefits deriving from olive oil's better resistance to oxidation at high temperatures. There are three rules to follow when cooking with olive oil: use abundant oil, don't use the same oil more than once, and drain fried foods on a piece of absorbent paper or material before they can cool off.

Above: *medieval print showing oil making.*
Center: *drawing of an old olive press.*
Facing page: *Olive harvest* (left) *and* Discobolus *by Myron* (below).

48 cruets

The idea of proposing olive-oil tasting in a restaurant—no longer a rare occurrence—belongs to the renowned *Enoliteca Ombrone* of Grosseto, which in 1978 first offered its guests a cart with a selection of oils to taste. The number of cruets on the cart steadily increased to 48, each one filled with a different fine extra virgin olive oil. It's come to the point where the gastronomic experts recommend that the olive oil should be matched to food the same way wine is. According to the rules, you should combine lighter and less fruity oils with delicate foods, leaving those with a more intensely fruity taste for heartier fare. In practice, this means using an oil from the northern Maremma for salad greens, a fruity oil from Chianti or Reggello for *ribollita fiorentina* (hearty country soup) or *cannellini* beans, and an oil from San Gimignano for *bistecca alla griglia*.

burned in lamps. Probably it was in the Mediterranean basin, the home of the Mediterranean diet, that it was first eaten. Today, the Mediterranean diet is being followed all over the world, mainly because of its emphasis on vegetable fat (olive oil) as opposed to animal fat. One of the first to embrace this concept was French chef, Alain Ducasse, who led the way for haute cuisine to fry in olive oil instead of seed oil. Olive oil is cholesterol free, aids digestion, and also favors the secretion of bile, thereby preventing the unhealthy effects of saturated fatty acids (such as those in butter or lard).

Viareggio and Versilia:
sea, Art Nouveau, and carnival

Versilia cuisine: *pesto* and *befanini*

People come to Versilia to eat fresh-caught seafish. (See "The Seafood Report.") A favorite dish is *cacciucco* (fish stew). Versilia *pesto*, a specialty of the Massa and Carrara provinces, differs considerably from that produced in Genoa because the local basil, *pesto*'s main ingredient, has a more delicate taste and fragrance than the Genoa variety. Versilia's favorite dessert is a platter of *befanini* cookies made of flour, milk, sugar, and orange and lemon peel cut into animal and plant shapes. Despite the fact that *befanini* are prepared especially for the "*festa della Befana*" (or Witch's Feast, as Epiphany is popularly called in Italy), they are available year round.

Viareggio, whose name derives from *"via regia"* (old road) is Tuscany's best known beach resort. Although it was settled in the mid 1400s, it became a township only in 1820, when Maria Luisa di Borbone commissioned its urban building plan. In 1861, the opening of the first children's summer camps marked the turning point in transforming what was then a fishing and shipbuilding village into a popular resort town.

In the outskirts are the **port**, the renowned **shipyard**, the wharf along the **Canale Burlamacco**, and the **Ponente** e **Levante pinewoods**. Viareggio's highlight, however, is the so-called "**Passeggiata a Mare**" (sea walkway) along Viale Margherita, which was originally an Art Nouveau boardwalk made of wood in keeping with the taste for the ephemeral in vogue at the time. In 1917, to everyone's dismay, the *passeggiata* burned down in a terrible fire and a concrete struc-

ture was built to replace it. However, not all the Art Nouveau in Viareggio was destroyed in the great fire. Several striking buildings such as the **Magazzini Duilio 48** and **Negozio Martini** (retail stores), the **Ristorante-Caffè Margherita**, and the **Bagno Balena** bath house survived.

Art Nouveau came late to Viareggio. Its chief proponents were an architect, Alfredo Belluomini, and a brilliant artist-potter, Galileo Chini. Among the famous Italians who flocked to Viareggio in its Belle Epoque heyday were playwright Sem Benelli, writer Gabriele D'Annunzio, composer Giacomo Puccini, and actress Eleonora Duse.

Above: *aerial view of the Versilia coast.*
Facing page: *Viareggio: Art Nouveau buildings* (center) *and making carnival floats* (below).

Marina di Pietrasanta · Lido di Camaiore · Viareggio · Lago di Massaciuccoli · Forte dei Marmi

Cacciucco *fish stew*

The best-known and oldest seafood recipe from Tuscany—or rather from Leghorn, the seafood capital—is cacciucco, *which is an elaborate fish stew. Although there's no set way to make* cacciucco, *most recipes call for a mixture of octopus, cuttle-fish, shrimp (cooked separately), dogfish, scorpionfish, waterhens,* spallotti, *and* traccine, *with sautéed onions, tomatoes, garlic, and celery. The fish are added in order of the firmness of their flesh. The stew is served over pieces of toasted country bread.*

A great carnival

Along with Nice and Rio de Janerio, the carnival of Viareggio, symbolized by its mascot, Burlamacco, has become one of the most famous in the world. For weeks, the city comes

alive in what seems like a never-ending parade of floats, band music, and confetti. The first carnival took place in 1873 with a procession of decorated carriages. To-day's floats, whose subjects range from biting political satire to whimsical fairy tales, are populated with gigantic motorized figures, which, since 1922, have been made of paper maché.

Puccini Lake

Above: monument to Puccini, *Torre del Lago* (left) *Lago di Massacciuccoli* (right).

The imposing **Viale dei Tigli** leads from Viareggio to **Torre del Lago Puccini**, situated on **Lago di Massaciuccoli**, not far from **Macchia di Migliarino**. The composer **Giacomo Puccini** (b.1858-d.1924) lived and composed most of his famous operas in Torre del Lago, where he alternated hunting in the marshes with playing the piano.

Today, his Art Nouveau residence, **Villa Puccini**, is a national museum. Guests can visit Puccini's tomb in the *chapel* and admire a life-size bronze statue of the master outside. Every year in summer, the city sponsors the *Puccini Festival* opera season in the nearby **open-air theater**, seating 4000, in honor of the composer of Madame Butterfly and La Bohème. Those wishing to explore Lago di Massaciuccoli can rent a boat or sign up for one of the scheduled boat excursions.

Forte dei Marmi:
summer playground for Italy's elite

The sights to see in *Forte dei Marmi*, for decades Italy's poshest summer resort, are a *fortress* commissioned by Grandduke Pietro Leopoldo in 1788 and a marble-loading *wharf* built in the 16th century. The town is actually a collection of gated villas surrounded by gardens and parks. During the season, which runs from May to September, there are attractions to tempt even the most demanding tourists—everything from antique, art, and flower shows to conferences and visits to artists' studios.

The town has numerous eating and night spots of note. One of the most celebrated is the *Capannina* night club, an elegant structure built in 1929 right on the beach, which is a favorite with the elite. According to those in the know, the Negroni aperitif was created by a Capannina barman.

Pontile-Moletto: *once used for marble shipments, it is now a pleasant promenade in Forte dei Marmi.*

Pietrasanta: antique, lovely, and white as marble

Pietrasanta can be described as antique, lovely, and white—in short, an ode to marble. Established in 1255 by *Podestà* Guiscardo Pietrasanta, it was taken over by the Medici in the 16th century. Thereafter, it fell into a decline which lasted until the 19th century. Its foremost monuments are the 13th century *Duomo di San Martino*, the *church of Sant'Agostino* which sports a remarkable facade with grandiose blind arcades, the *Archeological Museum* in the Renaissance *Palazzo Moroni*, the *Palazzo Pretorio*, and one of the oldest Tuscan churches, the 9th century *Pieve dei Santissimi Giovanni e Felicita*. Marble has always been the town's mainstay. Its *Istituto d'Arte*, where generations of *Pietrosantini* have learned the art of marble-working, is over 100 years old. It still attracts artists: *Henry Moore* was a frequent visitor and the Colombian artist *Fernando Botero* spends his summers here. Contemporary sculpture exhibits are often held in the town's main square. Take the time to make the climb to *Capezzano* or *Capriglia* to get a breathtaking scenic view sweeping from Pisa to Liguria.

Above: *Torre del Lago:* Villa Puccini, now the Puccini Museum (left) *and scene from La Bohème, Festival Pucciniano open-air theater.*

Center: *main square of Pietrasanta.* Below: *marble craftsmen working on the* monument to Andrè Bloc (left) *and foundry with Botero female figures and an abstract sculpture by Arnaldo Pomodoro* (right).

THE TUSCAN TABLE
Main courses

FLORENTINE TRIPE
(TRIPPA ALLA FIORENTINA)

Florentine-style tripe (cow's stomach) is cooked in its own liquid rather than in a broth.
Ingredients: tripe, sliced; 1 onion, minced; 1 carrot, minced; 1 stalk celery, minced; olive oil; tomatoes; grated parmesan cheese; salt and pepper.

Sauté onion, carrot, and celery in olive oil. Cook tripe for a few minutes, first adding sautéed vegetables and then tomatoes, salt, pepper and a bit of olive oil. Cook for 20 minutes. Sprinkle with abundant parmesan cheese and serve.

ROOSTER STEW (CIBREO)

Cibreo, which means Arab food, is not very common today.
Ingredients: Rooster livers, hearts, testicles, and crests, cut into small pieces; 1 onion, minced; 1 carrot, minced; 1 stalk celery, minced; butter; broth; salt and pepper. Sauce: egg yolks, lemon juice, and broth.

Sauté onion, carrot, and celery in butter. Boil crests. Add livers, hearts, and testicles and then boiled crests. Cook in broth with salt and pepper. Prepare sauce of egg yolks, lemon juice, and broth. Serve hot.

CUTTLEFISH IN TOMATO SAUCE
(SEPPIE IN ZIMINO)

Seppie in zimino is a kind of stew. The classic recipe is not made with tomatoes.
Ingredients: 1 kg of cuttlefish, cleaned and sliced; 1 kg of spinach; 1 kg of beet greens; 1 onion, minced; 1 carrot, minced; 1 stalk celery, minced; olive oil; white wine; 1 can of peeled tomatoes (optional).

Sauté onion, carrot, and celery in abundant olive oil. Add cuttlefish and cook for a few minutes. Add wine, vegetables, salt, and pepper. Cook for 20 minutes and serve hot.

MAREMMA BOAR
(SCOTTIGLIA DI CINGHIALE
ALLA MAREMMANA)

Ingredients: 200 grams of boar meat per person, cut into bits; red wine; carrots, diced; celery, diced; onions, diced; 1 bay leaf; broth; 1 can of peeled tomatoes.

Marinate boar meat in wine, carrots, celery, onion, and bay leaf for at least 12 hours. Sauté onion and celery in olive oil. Add boar meat and tomatoes and cover with broth. Cook for 3 hours. Serve.

FLORENTINE CODFISH
(BACCALÀ ALLA FIORENTINA)

Ingredients: Dried codfish; cut into pieces and dipped in flour; flour; onion, sliced; cloves of garlic; olive oil; tomatoes; parsley, chopped; rosemary; salt and pepper.

In an earthenware pot, sauté onion and garlic in olive oil. Add tomatoes, salt, and pepper. Fry fish in preheated olive oil with garlic and rosemary, remove, and drain on absorbent paper. Cook in tomato sauce for a few minutes. Sprinkle with parsley and serve.

TUSCAN BEANS IN THE FLASK
(FAGIOLI AL FIASCO)

Fagioli al fiasco is the traditional recipe for Tuscan *cannellini* beans. If you don't have a wood-burning fire, you can place the flask in a pot of water.
Ingredients: 500 grams *cannellini* beans, 6 tablespoons of olive oil, sage, garlic, salt and pepper.

Put a cloth on the bottom of a pot and fill with water. Put flask inside, heat, and let water boil off. Put beans, oil, sage, garlic, salt, and pepper in the flask, fill to three-quarters level with cold water, and seal. Cook for three hours or until the water evaporates and the beans absorb the olive oil. Serve.

MASSA

Massa, a leader in the marble industry and an important art center, is strategically positioned where the Apuan foothills slope toward the coast. First dominated by the Malaspina dukes, whose rule extended over three centuries (1400s-1700s) and then, along with Carrara, by the d'Este duchess, Maria Beatrice d'Austria, it did not achieve independence until the unity of Italy in 1860.

Most of the sights in Massa are associated with the power and glory of the Malaspina dynasty. Two of the most important are the splendid **Palazzo Cybo-Malaspina**, once the Malaspina family residence, located in the downtown area, and the **Castello Malaspina**, their imposing castle and fortress, which overlooks the city center from a nearby hilltop. Other not-to-be-missed sights are the attractive **Duomo** and a wooden *crucifix* attributed to **Michelangelo**.

Start your tour from the centrally located **Piazza degli Aranci**, so-called because of the fruit-bearing orange trees surrounding it on three sides which, in season, add an accent of color. In the middle of the square is a 19th century **obelisk** erected in honor of the d'Este dukes. On the south side, characterized by a striking red facade, is the **Palazzo Cybo-**

Malaspina, whose distinctive double-loggia courtyard is well worth a visit.

A short walk from Piazza degli Aranci is the **Duomo**, originally built in the 14th century, and extensively remodeled and restored over the centuries. The present-day building has a modern marble facade erected in the 1930s and a Baroque interior. In the underground crypt are the *Cybo-Malaspina tombs*. The remarkable wooden *crucifix*, regarded as a youthful work by **Michelangelo**, can be admired in the nearby **church of San Rocco**.

Before turning into Via della Rocca which leads up the hill to **Castello Malaspina**, admire the neo-Classic facade of the **Teatro Guglielmi**. The walled castle is actually a complex, comprised of a medieval **fortress** and a Renaissance **residential palace** connected by an arcade. From the many vantage points afforded by walkway atop the walls, you get a scenic view of the city below, with the sparkling waters of the sea in the distance. There are many worthwhile excursions in the environs of Massa. You can take a tour of the

Clockwise, starting from above left: Malaspina Fortress *overlooking Massa,* Duomo, crucifix *attributed to*

Michelangelo, church of San Rocco, *and Piazza di Massa or Piazza degli Aranci with its orange trees.*

Above: Palazzo Cybo-Malaspina, *Massa* (left) *and* Duomo, *Carrara* (right).

royal estates, foremost of which are **Villa della Rinchiostra**, **Villa della Cuncia**, and the grandiose **Villa Massoni**. Or you might enjoy hiking in the white (marble) Apuan Alps: to **Pasquilio** (800 meters above sea level), and then on to the top of **Monte Carchio** (1087 meters above sea level), or to **Pian della Fioba** (1000 meters above sea level) for breathtaking panoramas. Or maybe you'd prefer to visit the **marble quarries of Carchio** and Madiella, which are easily accessible from the town.

CARRARA

The historic town of **Carrara**, celebrated for its marble industry, is situated between the old Roman road, Via Aurelia, and the quarries. Once a free commune in the early Middle Ages, it was subjugated, first by the lords of Lucca, Genoa, and the Visconti of Milan, and then, like Massa, by the Malaspina, who ruled

Lard and chickpea cake

Lardo di Colonnata (Colonnata lard), produced in the town of Colonnata near Carrara, is exported outside Tuscany. Frequently served in slices on a hot fo-

it from the 15th to the18th centuries.
Carrara is probably the world's best known marble producer—and has been for centuries. There are two professional institutes where marble artisans and artists are trained: the *Istituto per il Marmo* and the *Accademia di Belle Arti*, the award-winning (for sculpture) art school located in Palazzo Cybo-Malaspina. Don't leave without a visit to the **Museo del Marmo** on Via XX Settembre, whose exhibits bring to life the history of the Apuan marble and the quarrying techniques.

The **Duomo** has a grey-and-white striped facade adorned by a remarkable 14th century *rose window* and a Romanesque carved *portal*. In addition to 14th and 15th century frescoes, the interior has a painted *pulpit* by the masters of the school of Carrara, a marble *vat* carved out of a single block, a 16th century *Baptismal font*, and the *tomb of St. Ceccardo*, the city's patron saint.

The loveliest square in Carrara is Piazza Alberica, whose slightly sloping surface is exquisitely paved in marble patterns. Of note is the building with a coat-of-arms. Supposedly inhabited by Francesco Petrarch in the

14th century, it was the home of the 19th century Tuscan historian, Emanuale Repetti, who wrote the authoritative work on the Apuans region's past and present.

Worthwhile (and easy) excursions from Carrara include a tour of the quarries, with the still-operating **Cave dei Fantiscritti** and the panoramic **Cave di Ravaccione**, and a visit to the old Roman town of **Colonnata**.

Top: *Piazza Alberica.*
Above: *Andrea Doria as* Neptune *by Baccio Bandinelli, Piazza dell'Accademia.*

caccia, it is made of pig fat seasoned with salt, pepper, cinnamon, garlic, rosemary, and other spices and "aged" in brine for six months. The aging process, it is claimed, enhances the nutritional value, flavor, and aroma, making it a versatile—and more digestible—product.
Don't leave Versilia without trying the lo-cal specialty, "cecìna," a flat cake made of chickpeas ground into flour, salt, water, and olive oil, baked in a traditional copper pan. Born as a simple peasant food, its popularity has spread throughout the whole region of Tuscany. Stop for a hot slice in one of the ubiquitous friggitorie or rosticcerie.

The Apuan Alps:
marble born, like Venus, from the sea

Left: portrait of Michelangelo.
Right: photo of Henry Moore in the Apuane Mountains.

The Apuan Alps, or Apuans, were formed 20 million years ago under the sea. Thrust upward by gigantic quakes, they emerged from the water as fossil-laden limestone formations that recrystalized into marble. Today, an incredible network of grottoes, crevices, and rivers lie beneath the Apuans, whose slopes are covered with forests of chestnut and beech trees and whose plains are covered with groves of olive and citrus trees. It is no wonder that such phenomena, unlike any on Earth, have always fascinated geologists and botanists, who have subjected them to the closest scientific scrutiny since the 1700s. More recently,

Marble for masterpieces

The Roman historians Pliny and Strabo have left us accounts of how the Apuan marble, quarried by slaves, was used in the construction of temples and villas. In Antiquity, the stone blocks were hauled to the Port of Luni, where they were loaded on barges for delivery.
Marble was not much used as a building or artistic material during the Middle Ages. Its decline lasted until the 13th century when masters such as Tino da Camaino and Nicola and Giovanni Pisano revived the use of marble for sculpture. By the Early Renaissance, it was again being used on a wide scale in the construction of churches, palaces, loggias, and fountains; special types such
as "Bianco di Carrara" (Carrara white) and "Statuario dell'Altissimo" (the Lord's stone) virtually became household words.
In the early 1500s, Michelangelo personally selected the blocks for his sculptures of the Pietà, Moses, and the Slaves. Interestingly, one of his never realized projects was to sculpt a gigantic figure running the entire height of a mountain to serve as a beacon for sailors. Still today, contemporary masters flock to the Apuans to select the marble out of which craftsmen known as "riproduttori" (duplicators) turn their scale models into full-size works.

starting from the 1800s, mountain climbers have set out to scale their peaks. By now, all—even the most difficult such as the **Sagro**, the **Pizzo d'Uccello**, the **Pania della Croce**, and the **Pisanino**—have been conquered.

Just as they represent nature, the Apuans represent the labor of those who, over the last 2000 years, have toiled in their quarries. Despite the huge advances in technology, the same technique—known as *lizza*— is still used in quarrying: The great blocks are fitted with metal harnesses and made to slide down the steep channels dug into the slopes. They are then sawed with motor-powered helical cables.

Above: *Alpi Apuane.* **Below:** *Alpi Apuane with clearly visible marble transport path* (left) *and the unusual double bridge by the Fantiscritti Quarry* (right).

Exhibits and events

LUNIGIANA: history, secrets, and good food

There are several fascinating museums in Lunigiana, foremost of which are the *Museo Civico Archeologico* in Pontremoli where the Lunigiana statuettes are exhibited, the *Museo di Storia Naturale in Aulla*, and the *Museo Etnografico della Lunigiana* in Villafranca. Since 1952, the *Premio Letterario Bancarella* is awarded to the year's best new publication by a panel of Pontremoli booksellers.

Right: fortress of
Fosdinovo,
Lunigiana.
Top right: *painted
wooden figurines, a
typical craft of the
Lunigiana region.*

The **Lunigiana** region comprises fourteen historic towns, of which Pontremoli is the most important, situated in the provinces of Massa and Carrara. The region was the feudal property of a dynasty of powerful bishops until the 11th century and thereafter ruled by the Malaspina family.

Our tour of the Lunigiana starts at **Fosdinovo**. Here, in 1306, Dante Alighieri was a guest at the **Castello Malaspina** that still dominates the town. If you want to visit the fortified town of **Caprigliola** just past **Aulla**, you'll have to walk, as there are no access roads. Nearby is the **sanctuary of the Virgin of the Snows**. The attractive town of **Fivizzano**, settled by the Romans, was subjugated first by the Malaspina and then by the Medici. On the main square, built by the Medici, is a *monumental fountain* and the **church of San Jacopo e Antonio**. Don't miss the **Palazzo del Governatore** and the impressive **Porta Sarzanese**. Next is **Equi Terme**, an attractive mountain spa. Of note in **Villafranca** along the historic *Via Francigena* is the

church of **San Francesco**. Nearby is **Filetto**, a perfectly square-shaped walled city with two symmetric portals. Our next stop is **Pontremoli**, the most important town of the Lunigiana, situated on the Magra River and, since 1952, the sponsor of one of Italy's foremost literary prizes, *Premio Bancarella*. Perhaps its most celebrated monument is the 14th century **Torre del Campanone**, erected by Castruccio Castracani in 1322 to separate the Guelph and Ghibelline sections of the city. In the 16th century, Montaigne visited Pontremoli; in his description, he extolled the town's cheeses and salads. After exploring the narrow streets and stopping to admire its 18th century palaces, foremost of which **Palazzo Dosi**, **Palazzo Negri**, **Palazzo Bocconi**, and **Palazzo Damiani**, walk up to the **Castello**, from which you get a panoramic view of the whole region. Inside is the **Museo Civico Archeologico**, where the **Lunigiana statuettes** are exhibited (sidebar).

The mysterious statuettes of Pontremoli

The prehistoric (Bronze or Iron Age) statuettes in the Museo Civico Archeologico in Pontremoli constitute one of the most fascinating riddles of Italian archeology. Many of them have been found broken: Some experts have theorized that they were smashed by the early Christians who regarded them as "pagan stones." Others believe they represent fertility gods, that were meant to be destroyed each season, or matriarchal figures, or funerary symbols. However, the only certainty we have regarding the statuettes is that they are related to the celebrated *menhir* and the Celtic traditions that were once widespread in the Lunigiana.

Testaroli: *Pontremoli's pasta*

Testaroli, the renowned specialty of Pontremoli, may be the original Italian pasta. Named for the "testi" cast-iron plates in which they are cooked, they are made of a dough composed of wheat flour, water, and salt. After being kneaded and heated in the testi, *the dough is cut into squares, triangles, and rectangles and then briefly cooked in boiling water. Lastly, the boiled* testaroli *are arranged in layers on a platter with* pesto, *olive oil, and grated parmesan cheese between the layers. Note that the* pesto *made with Lunigiana basil is more delicate than the Ligurian variety.*

Roman amphitheater, *Luni*.

Agriturismo

*A*griturismo in the Lunigiana means an unforgettable vacation immersed in nature, history, and art—at times in the company of sheep grazing amidst the ruins. There are rooms to rent, replete with all the modern comforts, in charming places like Costa D'Orsola, a stone-built village near Pontremoli whose attractions include year-round swimming, horseback riding, and tennis. Don't forget to sample the local cuisine—whose specialties embrace fresh vegetables, meat, salami, pastas. The fact that it reminds people of Emilian cooking shouldn't come as a surprise—the Emilia Romagna region border is only a stone's throw away.

The excavations of Luni

Settled by either the Etruscans or Romans, Luni grew into a powerful fortified port city. Marble and foodstuffs (principally, cheese and wine) were sent from Luni, not only by sea, but also down the Magra River. The city declined after the fall of the Roman Empire until the rise of the Bishop of Luni in the early medieval period. It suffered its second, definitive, downfall in the 11th century. Recent excavations have brought to light the **amphitheater**, the porticoed **forum**, and several **temples**.

Objects from the digs are on exhibit the **Museo** located in the Forum, the ***Accademia di Belle Arti*** in Carrara, and the **Museo Archeologico** in La Spezia.

Mushrooms and other Lunigiana specialties

The Lunigiana abounds with incredible gastronomic delights, foremost of which are "funghi pontremolesi" (mushrooms Pontremoli style), "pecorino della Cisa" (sheep's cheese), and "tordei" (pasta stuffed with aromatic herbs). Other treats are "bollenti," otherwise known as "necci" (flatcakes made of chestnut flour), "panigazzi" (unleavened focacce of wheat flour baked in cast-iron pans with long handles), "giasme" (focacce), "padleti" (flat rolls made of either wheat or chestnut flour), "spongata" (cake with honey, raisins, and pinenuts).

PISA

Pisa, a thriving port by Roman times, reached the peak of its glory as a sea republic in the 11th century. Its wealth of culture—and trade revenues—sparked a flood of innovations in art and architecture until 1284, when the Pisans were crushingly defeated at sea by its mighty rival, Genoa. In 1406, it was conquered again, this time on terrafirma by Florence.

Four genuine miracles of art—the Duomo, the Baptistery, the Camposanto, and the Leaning Tower, grace **Piazza dei Miracoli**.

The first miracle, the **Duomo**, was designed in 1063 by the **Buscheto**, whose innovative architectural style today known as "Pisan Romanesque" would spread throughout Tuscany and beyond. Buscheto (whose tomb is under an arch in the facade) never saw his grandiose project completed: the immense double-aisled building, including the facade, was completed two centuries later by Master Rainaldo. Bonanno Pisano crafted the celebrated bronze Doors of San Ranieri at the south

Caffè dell'Ussero: summa cum coffee

Located in an attractive terracotta-faced building, the Palazzo Agostini on Lungarno Pacinotti, the *Caffè dell'Ussero* (detailed in "The Coffee Report") is a popular hangout with the students of the nearby university. Among the intellectuals who have patronized it since its opening in 1794 are authors Giuseppe Giusti, Giosuè Carducci, and Renato Fucini.

The miraculous Leaning Tower

The Leaning Tower is still standing—or rather, leaning—after more than eight hundred years. Actually, the belltower's stability problems first emerged not long after construction was begun in 1173 by the renowned architect, Bonanno Pisano, who consequently suspended work at the fourth floor level. Construction was resumed in 1234 by William of Innsbruck, but the belltower was not completed until 1350 under the direction of Tommaso Pisano. Every year its tilt increases by another millimeter: At this writing, the northern end is almost a meter taller than the southern end: 55.22 versus 54.52 meters.

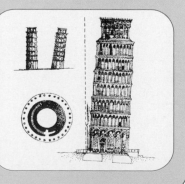

Mirror, mirror on the wall, is Nicola or Giovanni the best of all?

The two carved pulpits that changed the course of European sculpture are in Piazza dei Miracoli: one, by Nicola Pisano, is in the Baptistery (left) and the other, by Nicola's son, Giovanni, is in the Duomo. Nicola's hexagonal pulpit was sculpted in 1260 in an innovative style, combining naturalism and Classicism, that confers monumentality to the figures and architecture. Giovanni's Duomo pulpit, sculpted in the first decade of the 14th century, builds on his father's innovation, adding to it influxes of the International Gothic style from Northern Europe. The Pisanos' innovations influenced generations of Tuscan art.

Like gleaming white jewels strewn over the emerald carpet of Piazza dei Miracoli, the complex of marble-faced buildings comprising the Baptistery, Leaning Tower, Duomo, and Camposanto is a true miracle of artistic perfection. Individually fraught with historic meaning, the buildings may also be interpreted collectively as a symbolic representation of the Christian life cycle which, starting from Baptism (Baptistery), develops through reason (symbolized by the Leaning Tower, the embodiment of the perfect/imperfect dichotomy) matures through religion (Duomo), and ends with death (Camposanto).

transept in 1180.

The second miracle is the **Baptistery**, an impressive domed structure, which was begun by **Diotisalvi** in 1152 and completed in the 13th century. The result is a superbly harmonious combination of the Romanesque (simple central plan) and Gothic (decoration of colored marbles, gables, pinnacles, spires, and cornices).

The third miracle, the Tuscan Gothic **Camposanto Monumentale**, was begun in 1278 by **Giovanni di Simoni** and completed in the 15th century. Inside are unforgettable dramatic renderings in fresco of the Last Judgments and the Triumph of Death.

The fourth miracle, the celebrated **Leaning Tower**, which is actually a free-standing belltower, was begun in 1173 and completed in 1350.

Pisa is also a university town—and has been for over five centuries. It has two universities: the *Università La Sapienza*, whose origins go back to the 14th century, and the *Scuola Normale*, founded by Napoleon in 1810 for Italy's intellectual elite. The Scuola Normale is headquartered in Palazzo

Facing page: *aerial view of Piazza dei Miracoli with the* Baptistery, *Leaning Tower,* Duomo, *and* Camposanto *(cemetery).*

(continued on page 118)

Above: Camposanto.
Below: "Galileo's
lamp," Duomo (left)
and Via Santa Maria
(right).

On the north side of Piazza dei Miracoli is the CAMPOSANTO MONUMENTALE (monumental cemetery). According to legend, it was miraculously transported here from Mount Golgotha by Pisan Crusaders in 1203; according to history, it was built by generations of Pisan artisans who worked on the project for over a century starting in 1277. In the south end are the dramatic 14th century frescoes of the Last Judgment, Hell, and the Triumph of Death. In the treatment of the subject matter, they reflect the medieval views of the mysteries of human existence: Death, for instance, is shown as an old hag, who carries off a merry band of carefree youths instead of those in agony who are depicted imploring her to free them from their suffering. The frescoes are unsigned: Among the attributions are Pietro Lorenzetti, Francesco Traini, Andrea Orcagna, and, the most cited, Buonamico Buffalmacco.

Lamps lighting the way for science at Pisa

Galileo Galilei is undoubtedly Pisa's most celebrated native son. According to tradition, he made two of his most important discoveries on Piazza dei Miracoli: the law of the pendulum by observing the oscillations of the bronze lamp in the Duomo traditionally called "Galileo's lamp" (although today scholars agree that the discovery predates the lamp) and the law of gravity by dropping weights from the Leaning Tower. The **Domus Galileana**, a modern center for Galileo studies with a fine library, also has an exhibition of Galileo mementos. Along with many of Pisa's scientific institutes, it is located on Via Santa Maria.

The University of Pisa, known as La Sapienza (the learned), dates back to 1343 when the Studio Pisano was officially founded. It was expanded in the 15th century under the Medici prince, Lorenzo the Magnificent, who commissioned its headquarters, Palazzo della Sapienza, and again by the Medicis in the 16th century. It has one of Italy's oldest **botanical gardens** and a celebrated *surgery school*.

Above: Palazzo
dei Cavalieri
(16th century).
altarpiece *with V*irgin
and Child *by the
Master of San
Martino* (far left)
*and so-called Ivory
Virgin by Giovanni
Pisano* (left).

Three great museums

Pisa hosts three great museums: the **Museo dell'Opera del Duomo**, the **Museo delle Sinopie**, and the **Museo Nazionale di San Matteo**.

The **Museo dell'Opera del Duomo** in Piazza dei Miracoli was reopened to the public in 1986 after extensive renovation. The works on exhibit were originally in the Duomo. The highlights include **Giovanni Pisano's** *Virgin of the Holy Conversation* and the *Ivory Virgin*, and a 13th century wooden *crucifix*, as well as masterpieces by **Tino da Camaino** and **Nicola Pisano**. Precious church fittings and jewels are displayed in the *Tesoro*.

The **Museo delle Sinopie** in the former Ospedale della Misericordia was opened to the public in the 1970s. On exhibit are synopias, i.e., the underlying preparatory drawings revealed when frescoes are detached from their original surfaces for restoration and/or conserva-

tion. The synopias of the Camposanto frescoes, which were damaged by allied bombing in World War II, constitute a unique behind-the-scenes view of medieval artistry. Of historical interest are the 19th century watercolors by Giampaolo Lasinio which are an illustrated guide to mural painting.

The **Museo Nazionale di San Matteo**, beautifully laid out in 38 rooms of the former monastery of San Matteo has the world's finest collection of Pisan school masterpieces, from sculptures by Giovanni Pisano (13th century) and Andrea Pisano (14th century) to paintings by Giunta Pisano and the mysterious Maestro di San Martino (both 13th century). Other outstanding works on display include an *altarpiece* by the Sienese master, **Simone Martini**, dated 1319, and *St. Paul*, painted in the early 1400s by the Florentine master, **Masaccio**.

dei Cavalieri in the square of the same name.

The **Palazzo dei Cavalieri**, the **church of Santo Stefano**, and the square itself were designed by **Giorgio Vasari** in the 16th century on the site of the old Roman forum. The busts on the graffitti facade of Palazzo Cavalieri (di Santo Stefano) are portraits of the granddukes. In front of the building is a statue of Cosimo I de' Medici, who founded the religious-military Order of Santo Stefano in 1561, modeling it after the Knights of Malta. Inside the church, lined with banners captured from the infidel Turks, is Donatello's bronze reliquary bust of San Rossore, a masterpiece of Early Renaissance sculpture. **Palazzo dell'Orologio** on the north side of the square, built in 1607, incorporates the **Torre dei Gualandi**, the tower where, as Dante recounts in his *Divine Comedy*, Conte Ugolino and his children were imprisoned and left to starve to death.

Pisa has an outstanding collection of Romanesque and Gothic churches. **Santa Maria della Spina**,

Above: church of Santa Maria della Spina. Center: church of San Paolo a Ripa d'Arno. Below: Certosa di Calci. Facing page: *Romanesque* Basilica San Piero a Grado (above) *and the* San Rossore presidential estate (below).

The environs of Pisa: the Certosa of Pisa, the San Rossore Park, and the Pisa-Leghorn Canal

The celebrated **Certosa** of Pisa, an elaborate complex of monastery buildings erected in 1366 in the countryside of Calci at the foot of Monte Pisano, is well worth a visit. Its highlights include the church, hostel, cloister, Monastero Grande with its imposing Baroque marble facade, and the dining hall frescoed by Bernardino Poccetti in the 16th century. Nearby is Vicopisano with a tower, Torre della Rocca, designed by Brunelleschi (1406?).

San Rossore, a natural wonderland sprawling over 20,000 hectares, was known and appreciated by the

a profusion of tabernacles, gargoyles, pinnacles, and double rose windows, is a masterpiece of Tuscan Gothic architecture. Built in 1323 on the river bank, it was moved in the 19th century to its present location on the **Lungarni** (literally, along the Arno) for protection from the river's periodic flooding. Its name comes from the relic, a thorn *(spina)* from Christ's Crown of Thorns, that was once preserved inside.

One of Pisa's outstanding treasures is the **church of San Paolo a Ripa d'Arno**, which was built before the year 1000. Its striped marble facade is considered one of the finest examples of the Pisan Romanesque style. Not far from San Paolo is a striking octagonal building, the *chapel of Sant'Agata*, attributed to the 12th century master, Diotisalvi. Less than four miles from downtown Pisa (and well worth the trip) is the majestic Romanesque basilica of **San Piero a Grado**. It was built in honor of St. Peter, who supposedly broke journey here.

Romans. One of the Medicis' favorite estates, it was later owned by the Lorraine granddukes and thereafter by the House of Savoy. Today it is a national trust run by the President of Italy. The park is a nature reserve with rare plants and protected species, including deer, boar, and squirrels.

If you like the unusual, you'll enjoy navigating the old canal between Pisa and Leghorn. The idea of artificially extending the Arno to Leghorn to allow navigation between the two cities was first proposed by Leonardo da Vinci. Soon after, in the mid-16th century, the **Navicelli Canal** was dug so that goods coming from the inland could be speedily shipped from Pisa to Leghorn on their way overseas. During the brief boat ride from Pisa to Leghorn, you'll see the Tombolo pinewoods, the Coltano Estate, and **San Pietro a Grado**, with its splendid Romanesque basilica.

*Two historical water games
and a bridge to conquer*

*Make your visit to Pisa on June 16 and 17, the time of the fes-
tivities in honor of the city's patron saint, St. Ranieri. Since the
Arno River is the protagonist of Pisan folklore, all the festivities take place on or near the water. Walk along the river on
June 16, at nightfall, when all the facades are lit up, with lanterns
floating in the water to add to the atmosphere.*

*Two historic "water games" are played in costume. One is the
historic* regatta *contended by teams representing the rival sea
republics of Pisa, Amalfi, Genoa, and Venice, which is preceded by a stunning parade of over 400 people in historic costume.
The other is the so-called "Gioco del Ponte" (game of the bridge)
(above) which is a battle for Ponte di Mezzo played by two teams,*
Pisa di Mezzogiorno *(southern district) and* **Pisa di Tramon-
tana** *(northern district).*

The Pisan table

The Mediterranean Sea provides
fresh fish (as illustrated in "The
Seafood Report"), and the land, from
the mouth of the Arno at Bocca
d'Arno to the forests and plains of
San Rossore, is a veritable vegetable
garden. Fragrant truffles from nearby Volterra add a unique touch.
Typical Pisan dishes include stockfish with potatoes, anchovy pie, cabbage soup, wild boar, and baby eels
with peas. *Bordatino* is a favorite
country soup made of cornmeal,
cabbage, onions, garlic, creamed

bean, and bacon. The most popular
Pisan pie is called *"torta coi bischieri"*
made of beet greens, rice, eggs, bread,
nutmeg, grated cheese in a piecrust.
Traditionally served on All Saints'
Day (November 1), it can be eaten
sweetened (in which case, raisins
and pinenuts are added) or salted.
The Pisans affectionately call the designs on the piecrust *"bischeri,"* but
be careful about using the same word
in Florence where it is anything but
a term of endearment.

San Miniato, town of saints, countesses, and emperors

Rising on the hill as you approach San Miniato is the square **Tower**, a reconstruction of all that remains of the fortress built by Fredrick II in 1240. Until recently, the town was known as San Miniato al Tedesco because in the Middle Ages it was the residence of the vicars of the Emperor Arrigo, among whom was a German, Ruberto. Other famous visitors were **Barbarossa** (Redbeard) and Otto I, who founded the Palazzo dei Vicari, St. Francis, and Napoleon. Among the highlights are the imposing **sanctuary of the Crucifixion**, the 13th century brick-faced **Duomo** alongside of which is the **Tower of Countess Matilde**, and the **church of San Domenico**, with **Della Robbia** terracottas and 14th century frescoes by **Masolino**. There is also an art museum, the **Museo Diocesano di Arte Sacra**, which has works by Renaissance masters, **Filippo Lippi**, **Neri di Bicci**, and **Fra Bartolomeo**.

Above: San Minato al Tedesco (left) *and the* Matilde Tower *(Duomo belltower)* (right)
Below: *geothermic energy, Larderello.*

All steamed up!

An unforgettable sight is Larderello, an immense territory of dozens of natural steaming jets that blast from the earth up to seventy-five meters toward the sky. Larderello is Italy's leading producer of both boric acid and geothermic energy.

Alabaster in Volterra

White, transparent, translucent

Volterra is renowned for its alabaster, of which it has been a leading producer and crafter for over 200 years. First used by the Egyptians over 5000 years ago, alabaster is a rare form of chalk, sometimes translucent, found in delicate hues of white, yellow, or green. The alabaster craft was introduced in Volterra by Francesco Inghirami, the founder of the Museo Guarnacci. In addition to sculptures, the most popular objects made by in Volterra are plates, containers, vases.

Above: *Le Balze* (right) *and an alabaster craftsman at work* (left).

VOLTERRA
Etruscan enigma

Situated high on a hill of alabaster, Volterra has seen Etruscan, Roman, and medieval civilizations, all of which have left significant traces.

A walled city rising on a spur of alabaster, Volterra has been an Etruscan, Roman, and medieval center. For many centuries, it has been celebrated for the production of alabaster *objets d'art*. Its landscape and mystery have enchanted poets from Gabriele D'Annunzio to D. H. Lawrence. It has remarkable sights, ranging from the **Fortress** (now a maximum security prison), the **Palazzo dei Priori** in the square of the same name, and the **Duomo** to the **Balze**. (In Volterra, the word *"balze,"* which literally means "cliff," refers to the notorious rockslide zone on the west side of the city.) Our tour starts in **Piazza dei Priori**, one of the most beautiful medieval squares in Italy, on which stands the early 13th century **Palazzo dei Priori**, the oldest town hall in Tuscany,

a majestic stone building, whose facade is adorned with coats-of-arms. The tower affords a breathtaking view. Inside the 13th century **Duomo** are some notable works, including a remarkable wood *Deposition*, also dating from the 13th century and two 15th century works, a *ciborium* by **Mino da Fiesole** (1471), and a *fresco of the Three Magi* by **Benozzo Gozzoli**. In the 13th century octagonal **Baptistery** is an *altar* by **Mino da Fiesole**. The *baptismal font* is by **Andrea Sansovino** (16th century). The most famous of the several city gates is the **Porta Etrusca** (to which a Roman archivolt was added). Of notable impact are the ruins of the Roman city, which include the **theater** and the **baths**, and the **fortress**, which is actually a complex comprising two strongholds built in different periods.

Volterra has several fascinating museums. In

The Etruscan Museum of Museo Guarnacci

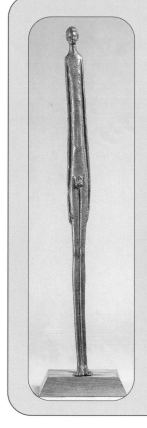

Although very little of Etruscan life has come down to us—no cities, no temples, no paintings—we have numerous examples of Etruscan burial places and funerary monuments. For the Etruscans, death was viewed as the happy destination toward which life leads, so the tombs were filled with a wealth of objects and utensils. The *Museo Etrusco Guarnacci*, one of the world's finest Etruscan collections, contains over 600 funerary urns in tufa, alabaster, and terracotta. Two of the most famous are the *Tomba degli Sposi*, with remarkable reclining figures of a husband and wife and the bronze figurine called *Ombra della Sera* (evening shadow).

Pinacoteca di Volterra

One outstanding masterpiece

The Pinacoteca has a small but excellent collection of paintings. One masterpiece stands out from the rest: the Descent from the Cross, *which is one of the finest works by the 16th century Mannerist painter,* **Rosso Fiorentino**. *The unnatural light and tension in the bodies convey an unforgettable impression. Other highlights include a late 15th century* Annunciation *by* **Luca Signorelli**, *the* Virgin of the Rose *by* **Taddeo di Bartolo**, Christ in Glory *by* **Domenico Ghirlandaio**, Pietà *by* **Francesco Neri da Volterra**, *and the* Virgin Enthroned *by* **Volteranno**.

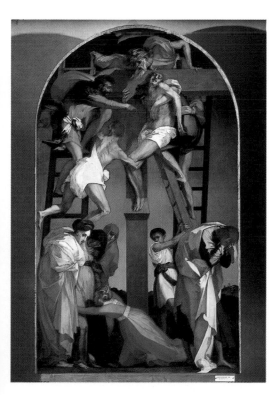

Tasty truffles

Italy produces only 100,000 kilos of truffles a year, which makes them both rare and dear. Characterized by a distinctive fragrance, they are *fungi* (like mushrooms) of the *genus* tuber that grow wild, mostly in forests, and are "sniffed out" by specially trained "truffle dogs." Popularly believed to be aphrodisiacs, truffles are found in three Italian regions: Piedmont in the north and Umbria and Tuscany in the central part of the country. The Tuscan truffles, found in the area around Pisa, Volterra, and San Miniato, are of the white variety, but there are also the even rarer black truffles, which are considered to be the best quality (below). You shouldn't miss the opportunity to try truffles at least once—whatever it costs.

Above: Descent from the Cross *by Rosso Fiorentino*, Museo Civico (left) *and black truffles from Volterra* (right).

Agriturismo

There are seemingly endless opportunities for a great *agriturismo* vacation in the Volterrano. One of the most unusual is a unconsacrated Romanesque church, San Lorenzo, which is part of a lakeside complex. Or you might prefer lodging in a five-centuries-old building in the beautifully situated Podere near Mazzolla, whose garden of aromatic herbs and

flowers is a rare delight, or in Ponzano, where you can choose between horseback riding in the valleys where pheasants, wild boar, and deer roam or excursions to the nearby art centers of Volterra, San Gimignano, or Pisa.

addition to the **Museo Guarnacci**, which has one of the finest Etruscan collections in the world, there are two important art museums, the **Pinacoteca Comunale** and the **Museo Diocesano di Arte Sacra**.

Near the Balze is the **Badia Camaldolese**, a church abandoned in the 19th century because of its vicinity to the rockslide zone. The Balze, which have been steadily eroding Volterra's territory for two thousand years, are a constant threat to the city's artistic and cultural heritage.

Above: Fortress, Volterra. Volterra: 13th century Duomo *(right) and* Palazzo dei Priori *(far right).*

THE SEAFOOD REPORT

Tyrrhenian seafood

The catch is abundant along the Tuscan coasts and Tuscans are well versed in the art of cooking seafood.

From time immemorial, Italians have been eating sealife. Today, seafood, regarded as nutritious and low-fat, is popular in many kinds of diets. The fish and shellfish caught along Tuscany's seacoast and in its numerous rivers and lakes are cooked in a myriad of refined ways. Among the most prized seawater catch are bass, dentex, whiting, umbrina, sole, and red mullet; freshwater catch includes eel, carp, river and lake trout, and, of course, salmon. The most commonly eaten shellfish are squid, cuttlefish, octopus, mussels, oysters, and langouste (Mediterranean lobster).

The cacciucco legend

In Leghorn, people have been eating cacciucco for centuries, but the recipe as we know it only goes back four hundred years, since two of its primary ingredients, tomatoes and chili peppers, were hitherto unavailable being native to the American continent. According to legend, cacciucco was invented by the guardians of the watchtowers along the coast who would fish during the day and cook their catch in a pot of seawater, together with garlic, bread, and a bit of wine, at night. They used olive oil supplied for their night lamps—with which it was forbidden to fry—to flavor the stew. The result is cacciucco.

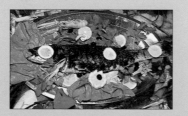

Dried cod

Dried cod, or stockfish, is made from mackerel fished in northern waters. Dried and salted for preservation, its taste is totally different from that of mackerel. Traditionally, it was eaten by the Catholic population on Fridays. Among Tuscan's famous dried cod dishes are baccalà alla fiorentina, baccalà in zimino *(codfish with beet greens),* stoccafisso alla pisana, stoccafisso all'agliata, *and the most celebrated of all,* baccalà alla livornese *(codfish fried with oil and garlic and then sautéed in tomato sauce).* Buon appetito!

trout

mullet

bass - languoste

sole

dory - umbrina

codfish

mackerel

Above: Fortezza Vecchia *by Antonio da Sangallo*. Center: *Scali d'Azeglio canal*. Below: *Terrazza Mascagni*.

LEGHORN

Out tour of Leghorn (Livorno, in Italian) starts in Piazza della Repubblica (Piazza del Voltone). Beyond rises the imposing fortress designed in 1590 by Buontalenti known as the "**Fortezza Nuova**" (or "New Fortress" to distinguish it from Antonio da San Gallo the Younger's earlier "**Fortezza Vecchia,**" or "Old Fortress"). The picturesque neighborhood between the Fortezza Nuova and the port, known as "**La Venezia Nuova,**" was named after the Venetian-type network of canals criss-crossing it. From Piazza della Repubblica, the arcaded Via Grande, Leghorn's main thoroughfare, leads into the old port, Porto Mediceo, that was completed by Cosimo II de' Medici in 1620. Nearby is the **Torre del Fanale**, a reconstruction of the tower built in the 14th century by Giovanni Pisano, which was destroyed by bombs in World War II. Only a short distance away, in **Piazza Micheli**, is the **monument of the Four Moors**, which has become the symbol of the city. Designed in the 17th century by **Pietro Tacca**, the monument depicts four Saracen pirates, enslaved and in chains, crouching at the corners of the statue of Grandduke Ferdinando I de' Medici dressed as a knight of the Order of Santo Stefano.

Nearby is the **Fortezza Vecchia**, a brilliant example of military engineering designed by **Antonio da San Gallo the Younger** in 1534. The fortress incorporates an imposing medieval structure, the 9th century **Countess Matilde Tower**.

Other sights include the picturesque **Bottini dell'Olio**, an usual 18th century structure comprising over three-hundred olive oil vats,

Leghorn, perhaps the least Tuscan of the Tuscan cities, is the region's major port. Its origins go back to 1570s when Bernardo Buontalenti was commissioned by Francesco I de' Medici to design an ideal city on the site of an old Pisan lookout. Throughout its history, its culture has been permeated with a strong lay tradition (significantly, the Italian translation of Diderot's Encyclopédie was published in Leghorn) and, like many great ports, has become a virtual melting pot of peoples and cultures.

Left: monument to Ferdinando I *by Giovanni Bandini with the figures of four* Moors *by Pietro Tacca.* Below: *Vettovaglie Market by Architect Badaloni (1893).*

which once served as a warehouse with a capacity of 24,000 barrels of oil, the scenic **Piazzale Pietro Mascagni** overlooking the water, and the neo-Classic **Cisternone**, designed in 1828 by Pasquale Poccianti as the city's fresh water reservoir.

In the centuries after its official incorporation on March 19, 1606, Leghorn, celebrated as the city of liberty and tolerance, attracted thousands of immigrants from the Middle East and Greece. Its status as a free port established in 1593 by the **Costituzione**

The art of cacciucco *making*

Leghorn's most famous dish is a fish stew known as "cacciucco." Its preparation is an art. Of course, you'll have to buy the fresh fish and all the ingredients at the iron-and-glass Mercato delle Vettovaglie designed by Badolini in 1894, which holds its place with the great covered markets of London and Berlin.

Cacciucco, which is actually a word of Slavic origin meaning "mixture," lives up to its name. It is made with all kinds of fish, including squid, cuttlefish, dogfish, catfish, scorpionfish, waterhen, cicada, mullet, not to mention purely Mediterranean fish known as "sugarelli," "sparlotti," and "sarpe." A simple recipe follows: Sauté a red onion, garlic, parsley, and a bit of chili pepper. Add a dash of Tuscan wine and some tomatoes. Add the fish, those with the firmer flesh (squid, cuttlefish, and dogfish) first. Cook over low flame. Pour over thick slices of toasted bread and serve.

Cheers!

The most popular drink in Leghorn, especially on a cold winter's day, is *"ponce scuro alla livornese"* (dark Leghorn punch), Strong as befits a city of sailors and longshoremen, dark Leghorn punch is made of coffee and rum, served boiling hot. The recipe calls for specially ground coffee mixed with rum distilled in Leghorn, and the mixture must be blended so perfectly that you can't distinguish the separate tastes of the ingredients—*"lo stacco,"* as the locals say. According to tradition, it should be downed in two swallows, but some prefer to sip it slowly. The most famous punch bar in town is the *Bar Civili*.

Livornina also made a notable contribution to its prosperity. In the 19th century, with industrialization, the Cantieri Navali Orlando shipyards were opened and more recently, in the 20th century, its coast has become one of Italy's most popular beach resorts.

To get a good idea of Leghorn—or better, of the *Livornesi*—you should visit the splendid modern Synagogue in the Jewish district on Via del Tempio or stop off at the colorful American Market in Piazza XX Settembre. If you like French Impressionism, don't miss the **Museo Civico Giovanni Fattori**, which features paintings by **Giovanni Fattori**, one of the best-known exponents of the Tuscan **Macchiaioli** school, that developed in the same years as Impressionism, but with a purely Tuscan twist.

Vespucci sails

Splendidly situated on the harbor, the Naval Academy of Leghorn was inaugurated by Admiral Benedetto Brin in 1881 shortly after the unification of Italy to train officers to serve in the newly founded Italian Navy. Over the years, it has gained an international reputation for professionalism and rigor. Its symbol is the Amerigo Vespucci, *the splendid clipper ship, which every year the students sail to ports near and far.*

La Venezia Nuova district (below) *and the* Cisternone, *the Leghorn water supply system built by Pasquale Poccianti (1828)* (far left).

Art and music: Giovanni Fattori, Amedeo Modigliani, and Pietro Mascagni

In the 19th and 20th centuries, Leghorn was a thriving art center. Giovanni Fattori (b.1825-d.1908), who was born in Leghorn, became the major exponent of the **Macchiaioli**, the Tuscan school of *en plein air* painting that is regarded as the cousin of French Impressionism. The name **Macchiaioli** comes from the *macchie* (spots) used to compose the pictures that have to be viewed from a distance to become "legible." On dis-

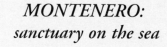

play in the **Museo Civico Giovanni Fattori** (Villa Fabbricotti) are outstanding works by the best known **Macchiaioli**, **Giovanni Fattori**, **Silvestro Lega**, and **Telemaco Signorini**. Many of the places that are reproduced in their landscapes may still be recognized today.

Amedeo Modigliani (b. 1884-d. 1920) (top), born to a Jewish family in Leghorn, left the city in 1906. He moved to Paris, then the center of the art world, where he produced virtually all of his great paintings and sculpture.

Pietro Mascagni (b. 1863-d. 1945) (bottom), the composer of famous operas such as *Cavalleria Rusticana*, was also born in Leghorn. Leghorn's tribute to him is the scenic **Piazzale Pietro Mascagni**, whose scenic splendor can be likened to the splendor of his notes. In the 19th century, when Leghorn was the most refined of Italy's resort towns, dozens of elegant bathing establishments such as the renowned **Pancaldi Baths** opened their doors; in those years, the charming *Palmieri Rotunda* (center) was designed by **Giovanni Fattori**. Then, in the 20th century, as Leghorn's popularity declined, Versilia became the favorite summer haunt of Italy's elite.

MONTENERO:
sanctuary on the sea

The 14th century sanctuary of Montenero overlooks the city from a scenic setting known as the Fiesole of Leghorn after the charming hilltown near Florence. People come from all over to pray to the Montenero Virgin. The ex-voto *offerings they leave when their prayers are answered are displayed in the Baroque church. After touring the church, stop off at the* Antica Farmacia *where liquors and honey produced by the Vallombrosian monks are on sale. (See* "The Monastery Reports.")

Map labels: Livorno, Quercianella, Castiglioncello, Rosignano, Vada, Cecina, San Vincenzo, Piombino, Golfo di Baratti, Populonia

The coast: Riviera degli Etruschi

Pirate early warning system

Strung along the Tuscan coast approximately four kilometers apart are over eighty watchtowers. They were built as lookouts for enemies from the sea, mostly Saracens and pirates originating from the Middle East and Turkey. There were two types of constructions: simple square or round towers with protruding brackets to support weapons or full-fledged fortresses such as Forte dei Marmi. The early warning system was controlled by the two fortresses in Leghorn.

The "**Riviera degli Etruschi**," the road skirting the coast from Leghorn on its way southward to Piombino, is remarkably scenic. The area is a paradise of transparent waters, a delightful climate, and verdant Mediterranean vegetation. Starting at is **Calafuria**, with its waterfront castle, the route passes through several renowned resort areas, including the charming towns of **Ardenza**, **Antignano**, **Quercianella**, and **Castiglioncello**. Contin-

uing past the industrial town of **Rosignano** and **Vada**, we come to **Cecina**, whose **Antiquarium Museum** has interesting exhibits of material excavated in the area. Further south are the popular resort towns of **Donoratico** and **San Vincenzo**. Nearby are the medieval ruins of **Populonia** overlooking the exquisite *Bay of Baratti*. A port and iron-mining center since Antiquity, Populonia was first settled by the Etruscans. The Etruscan necrop-

Above: rocky coast south of Leghorn. Views of the coast (right and far right).

olis, with tombs of several periods and styles, was unearthed in the 19th century. There is also a small archeological museum where the tomb fittings are displayed.

From Populonia, we proceed to **Piombino**, the port of delivery for the iron mined on the Isle of Elba—which is only a few miles away by sea. Piombino, first settled by the Romans, has some fascinating sights, foremost of which are the 13th century **Palazzo Comunale**, the **church of Sant'Antimo** (with some interesting sculptures and a Renaissance cloister), and a scenic terrace which affords a sweeping panoramic view over the islands of the Tuscan archipelago.

Inland: poets and cypresses

Some of the sights south of Leghorn have nothing to do with the sea. For instance, the town of **Bolgheri** is nowhere near the coast, yet everybody who's ever studied Italian knows about it and its avenue of cypress trees because they were immortalized in a famous poem written by Giosuè Carducci, one of Italy's great 19th century poets. (As a youth, Carducci lived in the nearby town of Castagneto, renamed **Castagneto Carducci** in his honor, whose walled castle, **Castello della Gherardesca**, deserves a visit.) A walk through the tall reeds amidst oak and holm forests around Bolgheri is a remarkable experience. It's a perfect spot for birdwatching and picture-taking. Our last stop is the beautiful medieval town of **Suvereto**, whose main attractions include the 13th century **Palazzo Comunale**, with its external stairway and crenelated tower, and the 12th century Romanesque **church of San Giusto**, with a fine Byzantine-style portal.

A must for gourmets
The Menu Museum

Italy's premier collector of menus and editor-in-chief of the magazine **Gran Gourmet**, Enrico Guagnini, has a collection of over ten thousand menus from all over the world, some of which date back to the 19th century. The menus are exhibited in his home at **Bolgheri di Castagneto Carducci**. Special exhibits are often held during the summer months.

Agriturismo:

Etruria on horseback

An *agriturismo* vacation in Suvereto means you can alternate lazy days at the beach with intellectually stimulating excursions to Etruscan sites in a supremely restful atmosphere far from the madding tourist crowd. When it comes to food, the local produce is fresh and delicious, and the olive oil and the wine are superb. Not far from Suvereto, between Leghorn and Grosseto, is *Sassetta*, where vacations combine the best of the seaside and the countryside. After exploring the area on horseback, you might well want a taste of the local specialty *"fichi sott'olio"* (figs in olive oil).

Above: *Viale dei Cipressi, Bolgheri.* Left: *Suvereto.*

The Isle of Elba, a riot of colors and fragrances, is shaped like a giant lobster, 27 km long and 18 km at its widest point, with 118 km of coastline. Although it lies only 10 km from the Tuscan mainland, it differs from Tuscany in many respects, ranging from geology to customs.

ISLE OF ELBA
So near and yet so far

Below: *port of Portoferraio, capital of Elba.*

The best way to tour **Elba** is by car. For convenience, we start from the island's major town, **Portoferraio**, which is a bustling commercial, fishing, and tourist port. Overlooking it is the Medici fortress, Forte Stel-

la, where Napoleon Bonapart lived during his first exile. Traveling westward, we pass the delightful resort towns of **Procchio** and **Bidola**. Next is the fishing village of **Marciana Marina** (Marciana on the sea), the site of one of the Medici-built watchtowers. The

road twists upward to **Marciana Alta** (upper Marciana) at the foot of lofty Monte Capanne, whose peak—and breathtaking view over the Tuscan archipelago—can be reached by a cabinlift. Returning to the

coast, we come to **Marina di Campo**, a popular resort with a golf club and attractive beach. Nearby are **San Piero** and **Sant'Ilario**, two delightful towns situated on the slopes of Monte Capanne, amid oak and chestnut forests. Continuing for thirty kilo-

Napoleon's pint-sized reign

Below: *Portoferraio:* Napoleon's Villa (right) *and the beach called* "Spiaggia delle Ghiaie" (left).

meters, we come to **Capoliveri**, rising one hundred meters above the twin bays of Golfo Stella and Golfo di Porto Azzurro, at the gateway to the island's iron mining area. Five kilometers to the northeast is **Por-**

to Azzurro. Overlooking the delightful tourist port is the 16th century **fortress of Portolongone**, now a penitentiary. We continue through the area where, up until recent years, iron was mined. Along the way, we pass the resort towns of **Rio nell'Elba**,

Having been granted the right to rule Elba under the Treaty of Fontainebleau, Napoleon elected to live his first exile on the island. "I made the choice," he wrote, «because of the mildness of both its climate and its residents.» During the less than a year he lived on Elba (May 4, 1814-February 26, 1815), he gave Elba a flag (for the garrison installed at Forte Stella), established a navy, built a network of roads, streamlined the government, and revived the mining industry.

Today, scholars from all over the world come to Elba to do research at the Centro Nazionale di Studi Napoleonici. *But you don't have to be a scholar to appreciate the mementos left by the great emperor on the little island. In the lower section of Portoferraio, his bronze funerary mask and a cast of one of his hands are preserved in the* church of Misericordia. *On the hilltop is the* Palazzina dei Mulini *(ring for the custodian), the residence that Napoleon shared with his sister, Paolina, and Grand Marshall Bertrand. Of note are the library and reception hall, as well as numerous Napoleon mementos and autographs.*

Five kilometers from Portoferraio is Napoleon's summer residence, Villa di San Martino. *In the dining room frescoed by Paolo Ravelli is the Emperor's distinctive "logo" consisting of two doves on a skyblue background pulling a knotted ribbon. The most interesting sights are the emperor's bedroom and study, with their original furnishings, and the Egyptian Room.*

Below, the Museo Napoleonico, *built in 1852 by Anatolio Demidoff, now houses an art gallery, the* Pinacoteca Comunale Foresiana.

Elba: something for everyone

Elba is a paradise for those who love water sports, from swimming to sailing. For golfers, there's a nine-hole course at the Elba Golf of Acquabona, open all year round.
For mountain climbers, there's the challenge of climbing to the peak of Monte Capanne (1019 m). For campers, there are numerous camp grounds by the coast. Hunting (red partridge, thrushes, hares, wild boar) and fishing licenses are granted as well. Elba draws scholars from all over the world whose interests range from archeology and minerals to the Napoleonic era.
Local festivities include the Campese May Nights, the summer blessing of the sea in Portoferraio, the blessing of motorvehicles, and St. Christopher's Day. The average temperature is 9°C (48°F) in January and 24.3°C (76°F) in July.

Above: *sailing in the waters of Elba.*

Sea food and earth wines

Elba produces an excellent white wine, Elba Bianco, and an excellent red wine, Elba Rosso, both of which have been certified Doc (origin controlled). Elba Bianco, a heady, dry wine with a minimum alcoholic content of eleven degrees, is served with appetizers and main courses, especially fish and white meat. Elba Rosso, an intense, fragrant, ruby-colored dry wine with a minimum alcoholic content of tzelve degrees, is served with main courses, especially roast and game meats. Excellent dessert wines, Aleatico and Moscato, are produced in limited quantities. The local honey is also top-notch. Unsurprisingly, Elba's cuisine is based on fresh fish and shellfish, including languoste (Mediterranean lobster), squid, dentex, whiting, and red mullet. Its fresh fruit and vegetables, especially early ripeners such as mushrooms and grapes, are luscious.

Rio Marina, and **Cavo** until we again reach Portoferraio. But don't think you've seen everything if you haven't seen **Fetovaia**, **Chiessi**, **Cavoli**, **Lacona**...

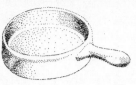

THE TUSCAN TABLE
Sweet things

RICE CAKES (FRITTELLE DI RISO)

Tuscans love *frittelle*—spherical pancakes made of wheat flour, apples and *vinsanto*, chestnut flour, or rice. Rice *frittelle* are most popular during the period around March 19, the feast-day of St. Joseph and thus Italian father's day.
Ingredients: 200 grams of rice; half liter of milk; two eggs (separated) plus two extra whites; 100 grams raisins; pinch of salt; 1 teaspoon of powdered yeast; 6 tablespoons of sugar; lemon peel; small glass of vinsanto; olive oil for frying; confectioner's sugar.

Serves six

Boil the milk diluted with two glasses of water and a pinch of salt. Add rice and, when the rice is partially cooked, add the sugar and lemon peel. Cook until all the liquid is absorbed. Beat egg whites. Add flour, egg yolks, yeast, raisins, vinsanto, and the egg whites. Fry little balls of dough in the heated olive oil until golden. Sprinkle with confectioner's sugar and serve.

TUSCAN ICE CREAM CAKE (ZUCCOTTO)

Zuccotto, the Tuscan version of ice cream cake, is a perfect dessert for an important dinner.
Ingredients: 50 grams of sponge cake, sliced into two one-centimeter thick disks; 500 grams of *ricotta* cheese (drained); 500 grams of cream; unsweetened chocolate, diced; 20 grams of sugar; 1 teaspoon of cognac; 1 teaspoon of dessert liquor; candied cherries and limes, diced.

Per person

Whip the cream with the sugar. Add ricotta and pieces of candied fruit and chocolate. Put the sponge cake into a round dish and moisten it with the liquors diluted with water. Cover with a layer of chocolate cream, then add whipped cream and press. Refrigerate for at least five hours.

FLORENTINE CAKE
(SCHIACCIATA ALLA FIORENTINA)

Schiacciata alla fiorentina is immensely popular in Florence during the Carnival period.
Ingredients: 100 grams of sugar; 200 grams of wheat flour (00 type); two eggs; 500 grams of lard; 1 packet of vanilla; 1 orange (with grated peel); 20 grams of brewer's yeast; confectioner's sugar; salt.

Serves four
Knead the flour and yeast with warm water. Let rise and meanwhile mix eggs and lard in a soup bowl. Add sugar, vanilla, grated orange peel, and salt. Mix dough for at least fifteen minutes. Pour into rectangular baking pan greased with lard so that dough is evenly spread (up to approximately a three-centimeter thickness). Let stand. Bake in a preheated oven for a maximum of 30 minutes. Cool, sprinkle abundantly with confectioner's sugar, and serve.

GRAPE CAKE (SCHIACCIATA CON L'UVA)

Since the prime ingredient of *schiacciata all'uva* is grapes, this delicious cake is eaten in fall when the grapes are harvested.
Ingredients: 700 grams of purple grapes, washed and dried; 200 grams sugar; 300 grams wheat flour (0 type); 20 grams brewer's yeast; 3 tablespoons olive oil; salt.

Serves four
Mix flour, yeast, and 3 teaspoons of sugar with some warm water. Add pinch of salt. Let rise for one hour. Roll half of dough into a thin layer and place in a greased baking pan. Evenly spread half of grapes. Add 2 teaspoons of sugar and two of olive oil. Add rest of dough and rest of grapes. Bake for one hour in a hot oven.

GROSSETANO
mountains, marshes, and Mediterranean

The Grossetano is the largest region in Tuscany, occupying a full fifth of its territory. A wild, stirringly beautiful land, it is a wonderland of mountains (Monte Amiata), hills (the rust-colored Colline Metallifere), and forests (covering much of the region of the Maremma; "maremma" being the Tuscan word for "marsh"), with over 130 km of coastline. Part of its territory is a protected nature reserve, the Parco dell'Uccellina. Its major sights include the capital, Grosseto, and the splendid towns of Massa Marittima, Pitigliano, Sorano, and Sovana.

Below ground are valuable minerals, which were first mined by the Etruscans. The abandoned Etruscan mines are like open sores in the countryside. Monte Amiata is dotted with dozens of grottoes filled with the fossilized remains of the tigers, rhinoceros, and elephants who once roamed the land.

Above ground are some of the rarest and most interesting plant and animal species in Italy. An example of the former is the especially fragrant variety of juniper known as "ginepro coccolone" that grows amid the "macchia mediterranea" vegetation. Examples of the latter are wolves and boars.

The Grossetano peasants had a hard life. Their responses were at times to rebel by following prophets such as Davide Lazzaretti and sometimes to become bandits like Tiburzi. However, despite the revolution brought about by the agrarian laws passed after World War II, there are still vestiges of the genuine Maremma like the butteri *and their herds and* acquacotta.

Ruled first by a local noble family, the Aldobrandeschi, and then by the Sienese, Grosseto was periodically abandoned when outbreaks of malaria decimated the population until the marshlands were drained and reclaimed by the Lorraine granddukes in the 17th century. The city that grew up in this striking land amid mountains, marshes, and Mediterranean is full of fascinating things to be explored and enjoyed.

GROSSETO

Originally a medieval castle, **Grosseto** expanded in size and population during the 11th century when the Saracens destroyed the nearby town of Roselle. After a long period of domination by the Aldobrandeschi, the town was conquered, first by the Sienese in the 14th century, and then by the Medici in the 16th century. Under the Medici, the marshlands were reclaimed and the hexagonal-shaped city walls incorporating the imposing Ramparts were erected.

The town prospered as an agricultural center during the 18th and 19th centuries under the Lorraine granddukes. A commemorative **statue of Leopold II, Grandduke of Tuscany**, rises in Piazza Dante.

Grosseto is a modern town with numerous historical sights. Among the highlights of its heritage are the Romanesque **church of San Pietro**, the town's oldest, and the lovely 13th century Tuscan Gothic **church of San**

Above: *detail of the* Duomo facade, *Grosseto.*

Center: crucifix *by Duccio di Buoninsegna, San Francesco, Grosseto.*

Below: Museo Archeologico della Maremma, *Grosseto.*

Francesco. Inside the latter is a great *crucifix*, which has been attributed to **Duccio di Boninsegna**. The **Duomo**, dedicated to St. Lawrence, was built by **Sozzo di Rustichino** between the 13th and 14th centuries. Its red and white facade is a modern reconstruction. Inside are notable works such as the *baptismal font* and *Altar of Madonna delle Grazie*, both by the 15th century artist, **Antonio Ghini**. The painting of the *Virgin* is by **Matteo di Giovanni**. Don't miss the **Museo Archeologico e d'Arte della Maremma** (in Piazza Baccarini) which preserves the objects excavated in Roselle, as well as bronzes, sculptures, urns, and a collection of paintings by Sano di Pietro, Sassetta, and Sodoma.

Take your time exploring Grosseto, gateway to the region, filled with history, nature, and culture.

Right: facade *of the* Duomo *of Massa Marittima.* Below: tomb of St. Cerbone, Duomo *crypt* (left) *and* Palazzo Comunale (right).

Above: *rock formations in the Colline Metallifere.*
Below: *Horseback riding in the lower Colline Metallifere.*

MASSA MARITTIMA
Antique, medieval, lovely

Settled by the Etruscans, **Massa Marittima** became a free commune in the Middle Ages. In addition to the oldest known book on mining, it vaunts three outstanding treasures: a stupendous *Maestà* by **Ambrogio Lorenzetti**, beautiful buildings, and the majestic, oblique Romanesque-Gothic **Duomo**.

Inside the city walls are several noteworthy sights. There are two museums in the **Palazzo Pretorio**: the **Museo Archeologico** (Etruscan art) and the **Pinacoteca Civica** art museum, whose finest work is the *Maestà* painted by **Ambrogio Lorenzetti** in the 14th century.

Outstanding examples of architecture include the 13th century **Palazzo Pretorio**, with a strikingly elegant facade with two orders of two-part windows and coats of arms, and the majestic **Palazzo Comunale**, in-between tall tower houses, with three orders of two-part

windows, and lastly the solid, but airy **Palazzo dell'Abbondanza**. For centuries, Palazzo dell'Abbondanza was the granary of the Sienese who ruled Massa Marittima until the town was annexed to the Grandduchy of Tuscany in the 16th century. Inside the **Duomo**, dedicated to St. Cerbone, are a grandiose 13th century *baptismal font* by **Giroldo da Como**, the *Madonna delle Grazie* attributed to **Duccio**, and the *tomb of St. Cerbone* in the crypt, which was sculpted in 1324.

The Etruscans? Later...

Don't be surprised if there are few references to the Etruscans in these pages about Grosseto. Turn to "The Etruscan Report" for more details.

In the province of Grosseto are two important Etruscan centers, *Vetulonia* and *Roselle*, as well as *Saturnia, Sovana, Statonia* (Poggio Buco), *Marsiliana*, and *Heba*. They give you a wonderful idea of the life and the art of the mysterious people whose origins are lost in time, but whose spirit is still alive.

Right: *red-hued rock formations in the Colline Metallifere.* Below: *horseback riding in the Colline foothills.*

*The red Colline Metallifere,
amid a paradise of minerals
from iron to pyrite,
are dotted with old and new mines.
And, from high, historic Gavorrano...*

The **Colline Metallifere** is a region of abandoned mines. From the time of the Etruscans, minerals such as iron, copper, zinc, lead, pyrite, and antimony were extracted in the environs of Massa Marittima and Gavorrano. Many of the hills visible today were formed by the weathering of piles of mine wastes. The view over the Colline Metallifere, with hues of red dominating the irregular terrain, is unforgettable. **Gavorrano** is Italy's ma-

jor pyrite producer. Inside its elliptical **city walls** are a castle and a superb 14th century *Virgin and Child* by **Giovanni di Agostino** in the **church of San Giuliano**.

There is also a museum of mining life, the **Museo Ricordo della Miniera**. Top-quality collector's minerals are on sale at affordable prices. You can also find *alberese*, limestone with antimony or quartz crystals, and many other minerals on your own.

This is the Maremma of the **butteri.**
It's one of the most scenic Mediterranean places, where geology, plants, animals, and culture blend in a untamed isolation of unequaled beauty.

Maremma exists in more than a geographic dimension. It's a complex, remote world, altered by man and at the same time uncontaminated, owing to recent land reclamation projects and its original characteristics. Here, the tourist becomes an explorer into the fabulous and frightening past, which paradoxically the modern world has not succeeded in eliminating.

Underground are the minerals extracted from the earth from the time of the Etruscans: iron, copper, zinc, lead, pyrite, and antimony. Above ground are the Mediterranean forests, surviving marshlands, pastures, reeds, lakes, intact wooded hills—such as those in the Parco dell'Uccellina nature reserve—with poplars, farmhouses, and haunting deserted beaches.

Shots of the Maremma:
Above: *cattle.*
Center: *Montepescali.*
Below: *fording a river on horseback.*

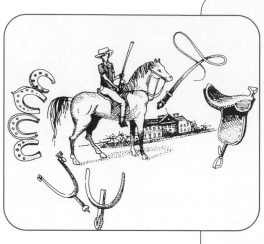

On horseback between woods and the sea

In the Maremma, not only the *butteri* cowboys ride horses. Tourists can go horseback riding around Alberese, at the mouth of the Ombrone River, near the scenic nature reserve, Parco dell'Uccellina. You'll ride the Maremmana saddle, known as the *"scafarda,"* which is designed more for work than for play. The horses are not among the most docile. The best riding seasons are February-March and September-October. You'll ride over grazing lands and waterways, taking care not to get too close to the herds of cattle. Take out your birdwatching binoculars every once in a while. You might sight a heron, wild duck, or hawk.

Here people—the last of the legendary *butteri* and shepherds—and animals live out their simple, quietly arduous existence.

There are wild horses, boars, water birds, and the immense cattle the **Macchiaioli** depicted in their landscapes. The fruits of this land are grapes for wine, vegetables, wheat, sugarbeets, sheep and cattle, and fish. To add to the multiple attractions of this untainted natural

The butteri, *Maremma's cow-boys*

From time immemorial, the buttero, *or Maremmano cowboy, has been a heroic figure, the tamer of wild animals. On horseback, he tames horses, brands herds, takes part in rodeos. He carries a long stick called "uncino," which he uses to open the corrals and prod the animals. He wears a small-brimmed hat, greased to make it waterproof, and high laced boots.*

His saddle differs from the typical English and western saddles. Everyone in the area remembers a celebrated horse-taming contest between the Maremmani butteri *and Colonel William Cody, better known as Buffalo Bill, who was touring Italy with his circus and cowboy. The* butteri *won.*

Left: *Maremma landscape.*
Below: *drawings by Fabrizio Pasquinucci showing two typical Maremma specialties: snails and lamb.*

King boar

Wild boars have always populated the Maremma. The Etruscans hunted boars on horseback. In the Middle Ages, they were identified with the devil. Here, protected in the thick forests overgrown with thickets, the wild boars thrive in the surviving marshlands. In winter, these unpredictable animals have even been known to come into the towns, especially Alberese. The legends about boar hunting abound—according to one, the packs increase in size before a war. At night, the boars, almost always led by an adult female, walk noiselessly through the woods in Indian file.

Maremma mangiari

Maremma, it has been rightly said, is not a place for vegetarians. Here meat is king, especially wild boar, which is roasted, stewed, cooked with fennel, garlic, rosemary, laurel, and red wine. Lambs, pigs, and birds also end up in the pot. Famous Maremma specialties are "scottiglia," a dish of mixed meats, and "buglione," a lamb dish. The Maremmani also cook exquisite dishes made of turtles (a soup), snails, codfish, and porcupine.

The Maremma is also renowned for the delicious beans known as "bastardone," "gaggio," and "lodola" that grow on the slopes of Mt. Amiata, even 800 meters above sea level and higher. Other specialties are a soup made of stale bread called "pagnone" and a seasonal dish, chestnut soup, known as "minestra di brodulose."

The region's best-known desserts are "birollo," a honey cake, "sospiri," made of beaten egg whites and sugar, ricotta pie, which can be eaten either sweet or salty, and "zuccatta," a marmalade of pumpkin

slices. There are also cookies, "melatelli," which are made of honey and hazelnuts.

territory is history, or rather, its vestiges, since most of the Maremma once was the territory of the long-vanished Etruscans. Here, in the heart of the so-called "wild" Maremma, at **Vetulonia** and **Roselle**, two Etruscan towns (discussed in more detail later on) created what would become the symbols of Ancient Rome's power and glory, the toga with the purple stripe and the two-part sheath.

Right: butteri cowboys.
Below: Parco dell'Uccellina nature reserve.

Pope Gregory VII, who forced Emperor Henry IV to come to Canossa, was born in **Sovana**, a stupendous town we shall soon visit. The environs are an incomparable medley of colors, animal voices, sea breezes, mountains, interspersed with steam erupting from the bowels of the earth. **Saturnia** has a popular

In the untainted enchantment of the Parco dell'Uccellina and other nature reserves

Opened to the public in 1975, the Parco dell'Uccellina, *named after the Uccellina Mountains rising on its territory, is a veritable paradise of seventy square kilometers stretching from Principina a Mare to Talamone. It is especially interesting for the variety of ecosystems it hosts: evergreen forests, marshes, dunes, and desert. The enchanting atmosphere of the park, which can be visited at different times and on different days according to season, is enhanced by the variety and rarity of the animal species who live wild in*

spa, full of grottoes with sulfuric water springs, and an Etruscan necropolis.

You can admire grandiose and isolated ruins like those of the Romanesque **church of San Bruzio**, built by the Camaldolese order around the year 1000. And lakes such as the **Lago dell'Accesa** (1825 meters in circumference), whose waters never freeze and whose shores, amid reeds, rushes, and bog-grass are populated with archaic fauna.

Above: *remains of the* church of San Bruzio, *Magliano* (left)*, mineral waters, Saturnia* (center)*, and the Lago dell'Accesa, which never freezes over* (right).

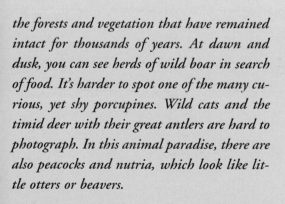

the forests and vegetation that have remained intact for thousands of years. At dawn and dusk, you can see herds of wild boar in search of food. It's harder to spot one of the many curious, yet shy porcupines. Wild cats and the timid deer with their great antlers are hard to photograph. In this animal paradise, there are also peacocks and nutria, which look like little otters or beavers.

Drawings of two of the animals commonly sighted in the Parco dell'Uccellina (deer and kingfisher).

From Torre di Collelungo, *we take the park's only road, and drive along 15 kilometers of deserted beach. An excursion to the Parco dell'Uccellina is like immersing oneself in a literal Earthly Paradise. And the sensation will remain impressed in your memory.*

Nearby are other reserves: the Riserva di Burano *near*

Capalbio, *where thousands of birds rest during their migration., the deer-filled* Parco della Feniglia *near the Aurelia, and the* Oasi di Orbetello, *which has dozens of species of birds such as cranes, red herons, and cinerini. All the reserves are near the beaches and historic places such as* Ansedonia, *filled with Etruscan vestiges.*

That long, wild, and fancy coast amid vegetation, sun, and sea

From the Golfo di Follonica to Castiglion della Pescaia, from Talamone and Orbetello to Ansedonia, with the jewels of Punta Ala and the Argentario

Drinking in Maremma

We've talked about food in Maremma. Now we'll talk about the wines to drink with the local specialties. Two white wines are especially suited for fish: **Pitigliano**, certified Doc since 1966, which has a delicate flavor and a low-alcoholic content (eight degrees) and **Parrina**, which comes from Orbetello, a dry, slightly tangy wine, with an alcoholic content of ten degrees. Another excellent wine is *Morellino di Scansano*, a ruby red wine, that goes down smoothly. The younger wines can be drunk with any meal, whereas the aged *Riserva* wines are more suited to roast meats, game, and stews.

Right: *mooring at Punta Ala.*

The drive along the Grossetano coast from the **Golfo di Follonica** cuts through the pinewoods between Piombino and Punta Ala. **Follonica** is a popular beach resort with a beautiful sand beach and pinewoods and an unusual building, the **church of San Leopoldo**, an eclectic structure of masonry and cast-iron decorated with Oriental motifs. Our next stop is the elegant resort town of **Punta Ala**, which has a little port, luxury hotels, and facilities for all kinds of land and water sports. Beyond Punta Ala lies the fishing village of **Castiglione della Pescaia**, now a popular resort. The lower section is modern, whereas the medieval section, which is walled and contains an **Aragonese fortress**, rises on the hill.

Having passed **Marina di Grosseto**, **Alberese**, the homeland of the *butteri*, and the enchantment of the Parco dell'Uccellina, we now reach a picturesque fishing village of **Talamone**, which is enclosed in walls and protected by a fortress. We then come to **Lagu-**

na di Orbetello (Lagoon of Orbetello) and the town of **Orbetello**, closed by the sandy stretches of **Giannella** and **Feniglia**. Orbetello conserves numerous traces of past history, from the Etruscans, Longobards, Spanish, and, in the 18th century, the Austrians and the Neapolitan Borbone. The **Duomo** is especially lovely.

But undoubtedly the most striking sight of this area is the high, rocky promontory of cultivated land, called "**Argentario.**" Once an island, it is today connected to the mainland by three thin isthmuses. The capital, as it were, of the Argentario is **Porto Santo Stefano**, whose two ports, **Porto Nuovo** (New Port) and **Porto Vecchio** (Old Port) are crowded with sailboats, motorboats, and fishing craft. Nearby is the renowned **Cala Galera**, with its

Above: *Golfo di Follonica* (left) *and panoramic view of Castiglione della Pescaia* (right). Below: *panoramic view of Porto Santo Stefano.*

What to take back

The *Grossetano* is a great place to buy souvenirs. Grosseto, for instance, is famous for leather goods. There's an especially good selection of riding boots and horse gear. Another traditional craft is *pottery*. You'll find an incredible assortment of decorated jugs, vases, plates, as well as glasses and bottles. Massa Marittima is renowned for *reproductions of Etruscan jewelry* and original settings for minerals. *Wrought iron* is another traditional craft. Collectors of antique weapons will appreciate the reproductions of *medieval crossbars*. Lastly, there is fine shipyard that produces *boats* in Porto Santo Stefano.

little port and moorings. To the east of the Argentario is **Porto Ercole**, which is dotted with Spanish forts. The great Lombard painter Caravaggio, who died here in 1610, is buried in the **Chiesa Parrocchiale**.

Having passed the picturesque town of **Ansedonia** whose Etruscan ruins will be discussed in more detail later on, we have reached the end of our voyage down the coast. The southernmost town in Tuscany is **Capalbio**, a picturesque medieval town enclosed in 15th century walls. You can climb up to the walkways, which lead into the houses, and which afford a breathtaking view. Every Sunday, Capalbio ends its summer season, with a renowned *Wild Boar Festival*.

Above: *bay of Porto Ercole and* Torre Stella (insert)
Below: *ruins of the Roman city of Cosa in Ansedonia.*

Giglio and Giannutri:
two Roman islands reborn with tourism

*The two islands, Giglio and Giannutri, can be seen from **Porto Santo Stefano**, the port for the ferries and hydrofoils connecting them to the mainland. The **Isle of Giglio**, which has a territory of twenty-one square kilometers, is the second largest in the archipelago. Its coastline consists mostly of jagged cliffs, interrupted by the sand beach of the Campese Golf Club. Its highest point is **Poggio della Pagana**, 500 meters above sea level. Giglio is a popular summer resort. The main resort towns are **Campese**, **Giglio Porto** (with excellent facilities), and **Giglio Castello**. Giglio Porto is a colorful fishing village, while Giglio Castello, located inland, has a 14th century castle and is enclosed in walls. The tiny (three square kilometer) **Isle of Giannutri** is the southernmost island in the Tuscan archipelago. It has few houses and hotels and is populated only by tourists in the summer. There are picturesque ruins of a 2nd century A.D. Ro-*

*man villa. For centuries, it was inhabited only by hermits. A lighthouse, built in 1860, revived it. You reach Giannutri from the north from the bays of **Cala Spalmatoio** or **Cala Maestra**, where there are still remains of a Roman port.*

Below: *Cala Maestra, Giannutri Island* (left) and *Fort San Giorgio, Capraia* (right). Bottom: *Giglio.*

The other islands of the archipelago

The attractions of the Tuscan archipelago do not stop at Giglio and Giannutri. The **Isle of Capraia**, a mountainous territory once inhabited by hermits, has a small year-round population and thirty kilometers of coastline. Visit the picturesque port and taste the fresh-caught anchovies. The smallest island

in the Tuscan Archipelago is **Gorgona**, which extends over a territory of only 2.23 km. Although it is occupied by a penitentiary, guided nature tours may be arranged. The legendary **Isle of Montecristo**, now a nature reserve, is composed of a single granite mountain, Monte Fortezza. It can only be visited by permission. Once a Roman summer residence, the triangular-shaped **Isle of Pianosa** alternates olive trees and vineyards with macchia mediterranea vegetation. Now occupied by a penitentiary, it can be visited only by permission. These islands collectively constitute the **Parco Nazionale dell'Arcipelago Toscano** (6000 hectares).

Tiburzi and Lazzaretti: two legendary characters

The Maremma is a land of free, independent, and nonconformist spirits. In the 19th century, it was overrun by bandits, some of whom were living legends as defenders of the poor. One of the most famous was **Tiburzi**, who for decades was king of the Maremma, feared and loved by the populace and chased by the police.

The memory of **Davide Lazzaretti** is still alive, especially in his hometown of Arcidosso. Lazzaretti was a religious reformer who preached a fervid, albeit confused, version of rural communism. He lived on Monte Amiata with his followers, the **Giurisdavidici**, who considered him a prophet and even a saint.

Thrown into jail time and time again, he was murdered by the carabinieri at the head of a procession he was leading down from Monte Labbro.

Monte Amiata: summer and winter tourism
On the borders of Sienese territory: a visit to the splendid medieval towns of Arcidosso, Castel del Piano, Roccalbegna, and Santa Fiora.

Monte Amiata, an active volcano 200,000 years ago, dominates southern Tuscany. The 12.5-kilometer hike to the top is well worth the effort. The spongy magmata rocks on high oddly contrast with the impermeable base, resulting in countless springs. The name "**Amiata**" comes from the Latin *"ad meata,"* or "at the springs"). There was never any malaria here and the mountain, divided up among rich landholders, gave work to generations of hard-working farmers and miners.

The environs are filled with delightful towns. **Santa Fiora**, at 687 meters above sea level, is situated at the foot of the **Castello degli Aldobrandeschi**. In the **Pieve di Santa Fiora e Lucilla** are splendid works by **Andrea** and **Giovanni Della Robbia**, illustrating the *Lives of Christ and the Virgin.* In the center of the medieval town is the **Peschiera**, from where the water of the Fiora River flow to the aqueduct. Nestled in-between Monte Amiata and Monte Labbro is the town of **Arcidosso**. En-

tering from the picturesque **Porta del-l'Orologio**, we visit the **church of San Leonardo**, with fine paintings and 16th century painted wood statues and then the **Rocca Aldobrandesca**, the majestic medieval castle complex. We also visit the **church of the Madonna Incoronata**, with its frontal ramp of stairs. After touring the lovely town of **Castel del Piano**, dominated by a clocktower, we stop at **Roccalbegna** which, on a tufa base, is dominated by two peaks, the Sasso or Rocca and the Cassero. The **church of Santi Pietro e Paolo** has noteworthy paintings by the Sienese masters, Ambrogio Lorenzetti and Domenico Beccafumi.

Below: *Santafiora.*
Bottom: *Arcidosso.*

Legendary "acquacotta"

*A*cquacotta (literally, "cooked water") is the most famous Maremmano specialty (though there is also an Arezzo version). Invented by the *butteri*, woodcutters, and coal miners, it was a one-plate meal made of practically nothing—which is how it got its Tuscany ironic name. Over the years, it became more and more elaborate. Today, it is served in all of the region's restaurants.

Nobody knows when *acquacotta* was invented, but why it was invented is easy to understand. Poor people who were forced to be away from home for long periods combined the few ingredients (water, salt, bread, and bit of oil) they had at hand and added to the mixture seasonal greens that they picked in the fields. Sometimes they had an egg, with stale bread and garlic, on top of which they scattered a bit of grated *pecorino* cheese. The dish was cooked in an earthenware pot outdoors over an open fire.

Today's *acquacotta* is far more elaborate. The essential ingredients are abundant olive oil, a glass of red or white wine, celery, chili pepper, cooked for an hour, and one egg per person. Other recipes call for *ricotta* cheese and even mushrooms.

Don't leave Maremma without tasting *acquacotta*!

Pitigliano, Sorano, and Sovana:

Three antique, solitary, and lovely towns

Agriturismo in paradise

Agriturismo in the Grossetano region means unforgettable vacations in farmhouses or cottages in splendid settings. Favorite activities are hiking, horseback riding, and excursions to Etruscan sights in the woods or along the beach. There are *agriturismo* vacations at **Roccastrada**, **Castiglione della Pescaia**, and **Scansano**. In the beautiful town of **Pitigliano** is a farmhouse with one hundred hectares of grazing land, with *Maremmani* horses. In **Marciano**, you can go swimming in the pool, barbecue your dinner, and practice archery. In **Capalbio**, the old barns have been turned into apartments with heating, burglar alarms, TV, telephone, and safes. The proprietors are always cordial, the lodgings are comfortable, and the settings are unequaled.

Pitigliano, Sorano, and Sovana are located at the extreme south of the Grossetano. The best known of the three is Pitigliano, *magically perched on a tufa cliff, with its monochrome buildings punctured by windows and doors like the underlying hills are punctured by numerous grottoes. In a marvelous atmosphere, Pitigliano has remarkable monuments, including the Renaissance* church of Santa Maria, *the* Duomo, Palazzo Orsini, *and, in the main square, the column on top of which is a little bear, the symbol of the Orsini family, who once ruled the city.*

Near Pitigliano is Sorano, *which is situated on a volcanic cliff that dominates the Lente River, amid tufa formations of striking beauty. Here, the visitors' footsteps can be heard in the silence. We start our tour at the* Collegiata di San Nicola *and proceed to the majestic* castle, *a fine example of Renaissance military architecture (1552), enclosed in overpowering walls interspersed with bastions.*

A short distance away is Sovana, *a noble Etruscan city that has survived twenty-seven centuries. In the Middle Ages, it was the birthplace of the powerful Aldobrandeschi, who ruled the region and gave history Gregory VII, one of the great popes. Sovana is*

Left: *main square, Sovana.*
Below: *interior of the* church of Santa Maria, *Pitigliano.*

filled with well-preserved mementos. The terracotta in the streets reproduces the original medieval paving. Perhaps the rarest treasure of Sovana is the ciborium *in the 11th century* church of Santa Maria. *One of a small number of pre-Romanesque works extant in Tuscany, it is supported on carved marble columns. Other medieval works are the* Palazzo Comunale *in the picturesque* Piazza del Pretorio, Palazzo Pretorio, *and the* Loggia del Capitano. *Lastly, stop off at the late Romanesque Duomo dedicated to Sts. Peter and Paul.*

Pitigliano, Sorano, and Sovana: three towns, three images that are part of multiform Tuscany, but that appear like a mirage outside and inside of time.

Below: *Etruscan tombs in Sorano.*
Bottom: *Pitigliano: panoramic view* (left) *and city walls* (right).

Events not to miss

In May and August, the exciting contest, *Balestro del Girifalco*, is held in Massa Marittima. On August 10, the feast-day of St. Lawrence, Grosseto holds a picturesque night-time *procession* with a statue of the saint accompanied by *butteri* on horseback. On August 15, Porto Santo Stefano holds the *Palio Marinaro*, a Spanish-style revocation of a 17th century boat race. Each of the town's districts is represented by a boat called a "gozzo."

The first Tuscans
Great and mysterious Etruscans

Fascinating tour among the ruins of the ancient civilization from which Tuscany originated. Places to visit and things to see.

Etruria extended over what is now Tuscany between the 8th and 2nd centuries B.C. At the height of their power, the Etruscans controlled a huge area starting from just below the Po River in the North to beyond Rome in the south. The Etruscan cities were first governed by a monarchy under the guidance of military-religious leaders known as *"Lu-*

Right: Etruscan relief, Museo Nazionale Etrusco, Chiusi.

cumoni" and thereafter as oligarchic republics. The independent city states of the republic (originally fifteen, then twelve) were joined together in a federation. After centuries of prosperity, decline set in around the 4th century B.C. The first to rebel against the Etruscan yoke were the Latium, Samnite, and Sabine peoples. Attacked by the

A Tour of Tuscan Etruria

The first stop on our Tuscan Etruria tour is a visit to the Archeological Museum in Florence.

VOLTERRA - The Etruscan highlights of Volterra are a section of massive city walls with a gate, Porta dell'Arco, adorned with three heads of divinities. A 2nd century temple and basilica are on the acropolis. The excavated objects are exhibited in the Museo Guarnacci.
SOVANA - The Etruscan remains in Sovana are splendid necropolises cut into the tufa rock.
ROSELLE - The scenic Parco Archeologico of Roselle, near Grosseto, comprises the excavations of

city walls and a group of houses. The excavated objects are exhibited in the Museo Archeologico della Maremma, Grosseto.
POPULONIA - Populonia along the coast was one of the centers where iron ore mined nearby was worked into metal. Among the most notable tombs are the tomb of the Flabelli, the tomb of the Colatoi, and the shrine tomb. The excavated objects are exhibited in the Museo Gasparri.
CORTONA - Important tombs and sections of city wall have been excavated near Cortona. Among the most noteworthy are the tombs known as "Sodo" and "Tanella di

Pitagora." The excavated objects, including the splendid bronze oil burning lamp known as the "lamp of Cortona," are exhibited in the Museo dell'Accademia Etrusco.
CHIUSI - Near the town are two outstanding Etruscan tombs, known as "Pellegrina" and "Leone." Splendid Canopic vases are exhibited in the Museo Nazionale Etrusco
MURLO - Murlo near Siena has an interesting archeological zone which includes a sixty-meter-long building containing around twenty rooms. Numerous painted terracottas are exhibited in the Museo Etrusco.

Etruscan museums

Museo Archeologico, Florence
Museo Archeologico, Fiesole
Museo Guarnacci, Volterra
Museo Nazionale Etrusco, Chiusi
Museo Gasparri, Populonia

Museo Archeologico, Arezzo
Museo dell'Accademia Etrusco, Cortona
Museo Archeologico Nazionale, Siena
Museo Archeologico della Maremma,
Grosseto

Greeks and Carthaginians, the Etruscans were defeated by the Syracuse navy at Cuma in 474 B.C. The final blow was the Roman conquest of Roselle in 294 B.C.

Although their language has been deciphered, their origins are still unknown. Some scholars believe they emigrated from Asia Minor, some from Central Europe, while others feel they might be indigenous people. Hard-working and astute, they

were great traders, artisans, and navigators. They devised ingenious systems for extracting iron ores, transporting them, and working them into metal. They thought they could predict the future by observing the heavens and the innards of sacrificed animals. What remains of their glory are the necropolises, or great funerary cities,

they built for their dead. Their art reflects eternal preoccupation with death and the netherworld: The early conception of the afterlife as a place of pleasures gave way to a gloomier conception of a hell filled with devils and demons. Among the artifacts excavated in the tombs are sculptures, objects in gold, silver, and bronze, and the so-called *buccheri* vases fashioned out of gray and black clay. The lids of the sarcophagi are carved with portraits, often of startling realism. Among the most renowned masterpieces of Etruscan art in Tuscany are the bronze *Chimera* in Arezzo, the *Haranguer* in Florence, the canopic vases in Chiusi, and the alabaster urns in Volterra.

Above: Haranguer, *Florence.*
Center: Funerary urn, Museo Guarnacci, *Volterra* (left) *and* Ildebranda Tomb, *Sovana* (right).
Below: *excavations at Roselle.*

Above: Two views of Piazza del Campo.

SIENA

A great story

According to legend, Siena was founded by the Romans and, according to history, it was subjugated by the Romans. After the 11th century, it prospered in trade and later in banking. It became a free commune in 1147.

For centuries, Ghibelline Siena fought against Guelph Florence: from the Battle of Montaperti won by the Sienese in 1260 to the final siege won by the Florentines in 1555. In those three hundred years, despite the Black Death, excommunication, and subjugation under Pandolfo Petrucci, the city managed to prosper. Its great artists, foremost of whom was Duccio di Buoninsegna, rivaled the Florentine masters, giving birth to the Sienese Gothic style, the first of the modern schools of painting.

Medieval in appearance by virtue of its city walls and in character by virtue of its seventeen contrade *(districts), independent and civic-minded Siena, which along with Florence was the birthplace of Italian Renaissance painting, is today a unique treasure trove of artistic masterpieces. Siena's noble history is entwined with finance, music, and cuisine.*

Sixteen palaces and other gems
Piazza del Campo

Looking like some giant, concave, irregular shell made of red-hued bricks ringed by sixteen imposing palaces, the fan-shaped **Piazza del Campo** makes a uniquely enchanting sight. Majestically towering over the square is **Palazzo Pubblico**, which is regarded by some as the most elegant Gothic building in Tuscany.

For centuries, the square has been the center of the public life of a city renowned for its civic mindedness and its independent spirit. The citizens would pour into the square by way of the eleven streets leading into it. There they would assemble to discuss public affairs, to listen to preachers such as St. Bernardino, and to attend festivals and games. Today, the **Palio** horse race is still run in Piazza del Campo.

As you slowly move your glance around the impressive sweep of facades overlooking the square, you get a feeling of great harmony. The harmony is achieved not only by the similarities in the facades (a law of 1297, for example, decreed that all the square's buildings should have three-part windows like those of Palazzo Pubblico), but also by the miraculous melting away of the notable differences in style and period thanks to the use of a single color exalting the harmony of the whole. Among the most noteworthy buildings are **Palaz-**

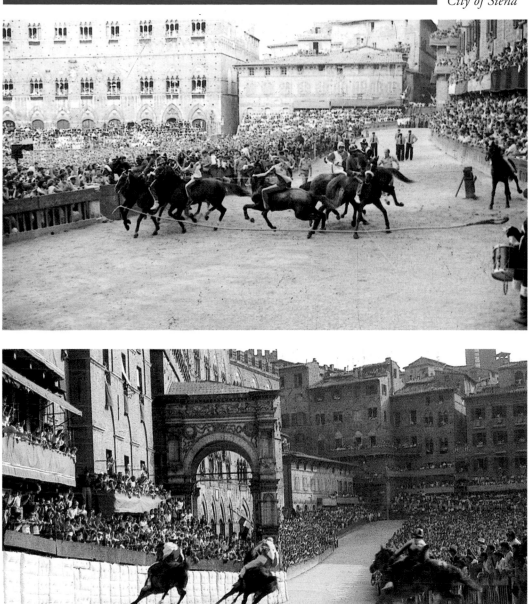

Palio, more than a festival

The **Palio** is not just a festival, a contest, a re-creation of a historical event in costume, nor simply a show put on for the benefit of the tourists. It is the religious and civil spirit of the whole city that, constantly inflamed, twice a year bursts forth in a great anthropological happening. There are records of buffalo and bull races being held in the public squares in the 13th century. The **contrade**, that is, the districts or neighborhoods to which the Sienese are fiercely devoted from cradle to coffin, originated in the 15th century and took the configuration we more or less know today in 1597.

The first **Palio** was reputedly run in 1632. In 1729, a decree established the number of **contrade** at seventeen, the same as today. The **Palio**, which is actually the hand-painted banner awarded to the winner of the race, is run on July 2 in honor of the Virgin of Provenzano and on August 16 in honor of the Virgin of the Assumption. Everyone in Siena takes an active part in the brief race which consists of three laps around Piazza del Campo. The horses are whipped into a frenzy by the jockeys who ride them bareback. Before the event, contacts are made, negotiations are carried out, bets are placed. Part of the event consists of a splendid procession of *Sienesi* in historical costume carrying weapons and banners. After the event, there are festivities and parties for the winning **contrada**.

Walls and gates

An inscription on one of Siena's main city gates, **Porta Camollia**, which is surmounted by lovely Baroque decoration, reads: *"cor magis tibi Sena pandit"* (Siena opens a larger [gate] for you). The city walls were built in the early 14th century not only for protection, but also as a sign and symbol of the city for its guests. Although they are built out of brick like most of Siena's constructions and are all in the Gothic style, the ten Sienese gates do not look alike. The most important are **Porta Romana**, **Porta Pispini**, **Porta Ovile**, and **Porta Camollia**. In the 15th and 16th centuries, some were adorned with frescoes by renowned artists such as Sassetta and Sodoma.

Above: Fonte Gaia *(19th century copy)* (center) *and* Torre del Mangia (far right). Right: Cappella di Piazza *at the base of the* Torre del Mangia.

zo Chigi Zondadari, which was rebuilt in the 18th century; the lovely curvilinear and red-hued **Palazzo Sansedoni**, the **De Metz mansions**; the 16th century crenelated **Palazzo d'Elci**, and the Gothic **Palazzo Patrizi**.

Looming above the **Fonte Gaia** and the **Cappella di Piazza** is the 102-meter-tall **Torre del Mangia**, the belltower that was built between 1338 and 1348. *"Mangia"* is the nickname of one of its former bellringers. Today, it would be impossible to name a belltower after its bellringer, since humans have long since been replaced by automated mechanisms that accurately toll the hours.

The **loggia of the Cappella di Piazza** was built right after the Black Death of 1348 in honor of the Virgin. It has been remodeled several times. Only the lower section is from the original 14th century building; the upper section and gate were added in the 15th century. The *altar fresco depict-*

ing the Virgin and Saints is by **Sodoma**.

The **Fonte Gaia**, whose name *"gaia"* (happy) might refer to the fact that it brought water to arid Siena or maybe to the fact that the Sienese were just delighted with its beauty, is located in the upper section of the square. The panels sculpted by **Jacopo della Quercia** which originally adorned it have been moved to Palazzo Pubblico. Free copies sculpted by Tito Sarrocchi in 1868 were put in their places. Water is hard to come by in Siena. The fountain water comes from an aqueduct twenty-five kilometers away which was erected in the 14th century. Among the rare public fountains, the most famous is **Fonte Branda**, which is protected by a structure consisting of three pointed arches. Built in the 11th century not far from the church of San Domenico, it was remodeled in the 15th century.

Treasures inside a treasure

Palazzo Pubblico

Inside the **Palazzo Pubblico**, a curvilinear masterpiece in the Tuscan Gothic style built between 1297 and 1310, are two of the world's most celebrated paintings: the *Maestà*

by **Simone Martini** and the *Effects of Bad and Good Government* by **Ambrogio Lorenzetti**—almost as if to contrast Simone's reli-gious spirit with Ambogio's civic spirit. The splendid—and ever harmonious—Palazzo Pubblico was enlarged over the centuries. The oldest section is the central core with the immense *monogram of Christ* (1425), which St. Bernardino took as his emblem. The first addition dating from the early 14th century was the **prison** on the right side. In the 17th century, a story was added to the lateral wings.

The *Medici coat-of-arms* on the facade (1560) commemorates Florence's defeat of Siena. On the right is a rampant lion representing Florence and on the left, the black and white banner representing Siena. A copy of the *She-wolf nursing Remus and Romulus*, which is the symbol of Siena as well as of Rome, stands atop the granite column on the far right side.

The splendid **Cortile del Podestà** in glazed terracotta leads to the **Teatro dei Rinnovati** (originally the Grand Council's meeting hall) and the Torre del Mangia.

Simone Martini's remarkable *Maestà* is in the *Sala del Mappamondo*. It depicts the Virgin enthroned amid thirty-two figures of apostles, saints, doctors of the church, and prophets. With his mastery of sinuous line and golden colors of enamel-like luminosity, Simone changed the whole course of Italian painting.

Facing the Maestà is the *fresco of Guidoriccio da Fogliano* attributed to **Simone Mar-**

Left: *engraving of* Palazzo Pubblico. Below: Palazzo Pubblico*:* Maestà *by Simone Martini (early 14th century)* (left) *and* Allegory of Good Government *by Ambrogio Lorenzetti (1338-1340).*

tini. The scene shows the rider and his horse harmoniously and rhythmically crossing through the naturalistic, yet storybook land-

Right: Guidoricco da Fogliano Besieging Montemassi *attributed to Simone Martini*, Palazzo Pubblico *(1328).*

scape surrounding the castles conquered by Guidorricio.

Ambrogio Lorenzetti painted the frescos of the *Effects of Good Government in the City and the Country* and the *Effects of Bad Government* on three walls between 1338 and 1340 as a tribute to the Republic's Government of the Nine. The allegory on the middle wall represents Good Government.

Sienese cuisine

And, for a first course, peachy pici

Pici, *perhaps Siena's most representative dish, makes a mythical first course (although there are numerous variations of* pici *in Casentino and Umbria).* Pici *are homemade spaghetti whose sole ingredients are wheat flour and water. Three characteristics distinguish* pici *from other kinds of pastas: One, unlike* tagliatelle, *they have no egg. Two, unlike machine-made pasta, they are not dried out, but are cooked fresh daily. Three, unlike most pasta, they are appreciated for their irregular size. They are of different lengths (up to forty centimeters) and diameters because, having been cut into long strips and flattened in a wooden form, they are are manually shaped. The name* pici *derives from "appicciare," which translated from the Sienese dialect means "to round out." Pici are served with virtually any sauce: "con le briciole" (with hot bread crumbs), fresh tomatoes, meat sauce, goose, hare, mushrooms, all of which are sprinkled with fragrant* pecorino delle Crete. *For those who like it hot, there's the Tuscan* aglione *sauce, which is garlic sautéed in hot olive oil with a bit of tomato and chili pepper. You can cool down your throat with a glass of one of the excellent local wines. As you travel around the Sienese region, you'll find* pici *under different names such as "ceriole," "lunghetti," "stringozzi," and "strozzapreti".*

Left: Duomo. *The lower part of the facade is by Giovanni Pisano (1284-1296).*

The religious center

The Duomo and the Baptistery

Piccolomini Library: A pope, a painter, and illuminated manuscripts galore

The splendid **Duomo** of Siena is proof that a masterpiece may be born out of contrast and contradiction. The facade, which celebrates the Virgin, the guardian of Siena, is itself a contrast: The lower section is Romanesque, attributed to Giovanni Pisano and perhaps also to Tino di Camaino, while the upper section is International Style. The essential parts of the church were already up by the mid-13th century. But the Sienese wanted to outdo their rivals, the Florentines; they wanted their cathedral to be bigger and better than the Duomo of Florence. In 1317, when an enlargement proposed by Camaino di Crescentino was rejected, it was decided instead to enlarge the whole building. Under the new plan, the existing building was to be only one

The Piccolomini Library was founded in 1495 to commemorate the great Humanist Pope Pius II Piccolomini and to preserve his library. The splendid rectangular room was entirely frescoed by Pinturicchio from 1502 to 1509 with scenes from the Pope's life. Most of the stupendous illuminated manuscripts were originally part of the Duomo collection.

Below: pulpit by Nicola Pisano, Duomo (1265-1268).

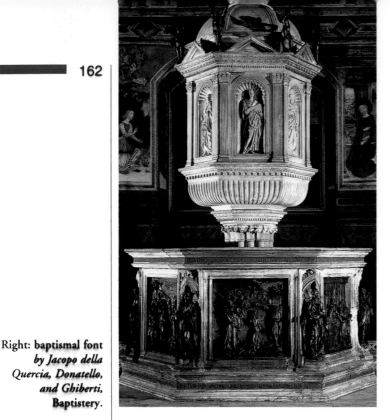

Right: baptismal font by Jacopo della Quercia, Donatello, and Ghiberti, Baptistery.

The spacious, color-filled interior has a stupendous relief flooring and two remarkable *holy water fonts*. But the greatest masterpiece by far is the octagonal *pulpit*, supported by three-lobed arches, carved by **Nicola Pisano** and **Arnolfo di Cambio**. Other highlights include the 17th century *Cappella del Voto* and the Renaissance *Cappella di San Giovanni Battista*. The grandiose *Piccolomini Altar*, a 15th century work by **Andrea Bregno**, dominates the left aisle. The entrance to the **Piccolomini Library** is in the Duomo.

The **Baptistery** has a remarkable 14th century facade with three elegant portals. The upper section was never completed. The interior is a treasure trove of Early Renaissance sculpture: the *baptismal font* and *St. John the Baptist* are by **Jacopo della Quercia**, the *bronze angels* are by **Donatello**, and the six *gilded bronze panels with scenes from the life of John the Baptist* are by **Jacopo della Quercia**, **Donatello**, and **Lorenzo Ghiberti**.

of the transepts of a much larger church. With the advent of the Black Death in 1348, the plans were dropped and the project was left as we see it today.

Below: Fainting of St. Catherine by Sodoma, San Domenico (left) and St. Catherine's house (right).

The House of St. Catherine: Sienese and patron of Italy

Visiting the house of a saint makes one reflect. The birthplace of St. Catherine of Siena, who was born in 1347 and who died in 1380, is on a narrow street, Vicolo del Tiratoio, next to the Fonte Branda. You can visit the great sanctuary, *the* Upper Oratory (kitchen), *the* Lower Oratory, *the* Chamber Oratory, *and* church of the Crucifix. *In addition to the remains of the original fireplace and other mementos of the saint, the exhibits include seventeen paintings representing scenes from her life. Her personal objects (including the stone she used as a pillow) are displayed in the nearby* cell. *Canonized in 1461, St. Catherine was proclaimed patron saint of Italy in 1939.*

Two great saints, two great churches

San Francesco and San Domenico

Siena's cityscape is characterized by by two immense churches: the 14th century **church of San Francesco** dedicated to St. Francis and the 13th century **church of San Domenico** dedicated to St. Dominic. **San Domenico**, built in the French Cistercian style, was begun in 1225 and completed over two hundred years later. In a certain sense, it is the church of St. Catherine, because, it is said, it is where she would pray. Over the altar is the *portrait of the saint* believed to bear the closest resemblance. It was painted by **Andrea Vanni** who knew her personally. On either side of the main altar are two lovely *candelabra angels* sculpted by **Benedetto da Maiano**.
The Gothic **basilica of San Francesco** has a fine brick facade with an impressive *portal* and a splendid *rose window*. The majestic interior is aisleless. There are two noteworthy tombs: the 13th century *tomb of the Tolomei* and the 15th century *tomb of Cristoforo Felici*. Of note is the *Crucifixion*, characterized by an abstract, desperate sweetness, which **Pietro Lorenzetti** painted in 1331.

Inside the two churches, Siena, city of faith and mysticism, achieves a synthesis that time has not altered. Outside, the palaces and towers reflect the face of the civic-minded city

Above: basilica of San Francesco *(1326): Interior* (left) *and* Crucifixion *by Pietro Lorenzetti.* Below: basilica di San Domenico *(1225).*

Masterpieces of the Museo dell'Opera del Duomo

One of the great masterpieces of Western art, the **Maestà** painted by **Duccio di Boninsegna** between 1308 and 1311, is in the **Museo dell'Opera del Duomo**. The work was acclaimed by the entire populace of Siena when it was moved from the artist's studio to the Duomo, where it was kept for two hundred years. Originally painted on both sides, it is composed of sixty panels with scenes of the life of Christ and the Virgin, and figures of prophets and apostles. In the 18th century, the two sides were separated. Since 1878, it has been displayed in the Museo dell'Opera del Duomo. The work is majestic, not only because of the Virgin majestically enthroned (i.e., **Maestà**), but because everything in it contributes to emphasizing the stateliness of the figure of the Virgin who, with her dark cloak, stands out of the gold ground. In keeping with the old Sienese mystic tradition, the predellas, with their bright colors and lively compositions, emanate a calm sweetness.

There are other noteworthy works in the museum, including **Pietro Lorenzetti's** masterpiece **Nativity of the Virgin** dated 1342, a youthful **Virgin** by **Duccio**, as well as sculpture by **Giovanni Pisano** and **Jacopo della Quercia**.

Above: *Duccio di Boninsegna:* Maestà *(1308-1311)* (left) *and the* Virgin of the Francescani (right).

Below: Nativity of the Virgin *by Pietro Lorenzetti (1342)* (left) *and* Townscape *by Ambrogio Lorenzetti* (right).

Masterpieces of the Pinacoteca Nazionale

One of the world's great collection of Italian art, the **Pinacoteca Nazionale** is in the fine Gothic-style **Palazzo Buonsignori** (1440). Among its treasures are two panel paintings attributed to **Ambrogio Lorenzetti** depicting a **Lakeside Castle** and a **Marine Townscape**, which are among the earliest examples of Italian landscape painting. The museum's pride are three paintings of the Virgin: the **Virgin and Child with Saints and Angels** by **Ambrogio Lorenzetti**, the **Virgin of the Franciscans** by **Duccio di Boninsegna**, and the **Virgin and Child** by **Simone Martini**. The collection includes fine works by **Pinturicchio**, **Dürer**, and **Lorenzo Lotto**.

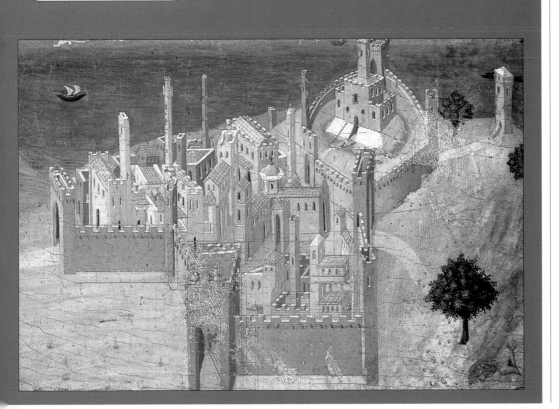

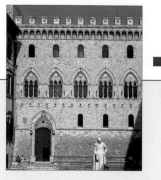

Music for the world
The Accademia Chigiana

Siena is the proud home of the celebrated music school, the Accademia Chigiana. It was founded in 1932 by Count Guido Chigi Saracini who donated his family palace as its headquarters (left). The world's most celebrated composers and musicians, including Alfredo Casella, Andres Segovia, and Paul van Kem-pen, have played or taught here. Stu-dents are admitted to the prestigious summer school courses *only after passing a tough se-lection process. Over forty coun-tries are represent-ed. The Accademia also is a famous* opera school. *Every year the term ends with the popular concerts of the* Sienese Musical Weeks. *The music is gener-ally selected from the works of one of the lesser known Italian composers of the 16th through 18th centuries. The Quintetto Chigiano, founded in 1939, is also well-known by music lovers.*

Centuries of safe deposit
Monte dei Paschi

Having been founded in 1472, Monte dei Paschi di Siena undoubtedly ranks as one of the oldest banks in the world. And it intends to ensure that Siena, a leader in European banking and finance during the Middle Ages and the Renaissance, remains at the fore-front in today's European Union. Originating from the Sienese economic humus; Monte dei Paschi di Siena was established by the Republican city gov-ernment, according to its bylaws, "ad provedere che le povere o miserabili persone sieno aiutate e subevenute" ("to help the poor and needy of Siena"). Since 1624, when the Grandduke of Tuscany grant-ed the bank the grazing rights to the Maremma ter-ritory, the bank has continued to grow. What makes it so unusual is the close relationship it has developed with the city of Siena, from which it receives much and to which it gives much.

SPECIAL TOUR
OF SIENA'S GREAT PALACES

One of the most oldest (1205) and loveliest private palaces in Siena is the stone-hewn Gothic **Palazzo Tolomei** (right) on Via Banchi Di Sopra. Built in the Gothic style, it has splendid two-part windows. On Via Banchi di Sotto is one of **Bernardo Rossellino's** Re-naissance masterpieces, **Palazzo Piccolomini** (left), with a splendid cornice reminiscent of Palazzo Rucellai in Florence. Inside is a stu-pendous collection of Sienese Biccherne.

Sienese sweets

For centuries, panforte, ricciarelli, cavallucci, *and* copate have been Siena's sweeties.

Siena's renowned sweets have been popular for centuries— in not only in Siena. They're "sweets" rather than "desserts" because during the Middle Ages and the Renaissance, they were eaten throughout the meal and not just at the end. Round panforte *cakes, perhaps the most famous, are made of candied fruit, honey, almonds, and Oriental spices. According to tradition, the recipe was invented by cloistered nuns. Some say that* panes melatos, *with* panpepato *the precursor of* panforte, *even goes back to Dante's time. The chronicles mention* "panpepati, biricuocoli, cupate et marzapanetti alla senese." *Today* biricuocoli *are known as* cavallucci *(horses) after the design on their crust (the chewy spicy cakes were popular breakfast cakes at the 19th century outpost* *stations).* Marzapanetti *are today's ricciarelli, crumbly little almond cakes covered with confectioner's sugar.* Copate, *as the cupate are called today, are believed to be of medieval origin, although some scholars have traced them back to the pre-Roman era. Probably they originated from a Sicilian cake which in turn originated from an Arabic recipe, since* "copata" *means almond cake in Arabic. The* copate, *made of almonds, honey, nuts, eggs, anise, and sugar, with a wafer covering, are white, although there were once* "cupate nere" *(black copate) made with chocolate. In Siena, you'll find freshly baked* panforte, ricciarelli, cavallucci, *and* copate. *But you don't have to go to Siena to eat these marvelous treats: They are exported all over the world.*

Above: *Sienese pastry chef preparing the traditional* panforte *dessert.*
Center: panforte *cut into* cavallucci *cookies in the center and* ricciarelli *cookies on the right* (above) *and old engraving of* panforte *preparation.*

Colle Val d'Elsa: medieval and crystal

If you appreciate fine glassware and the glitter of crystal, make a visit to the lovely town of Colle Val d'Elsa. The medieval section is on the hill; the modern section spreads over the valley. You enter the medieval walled town by way of the 16th century **Palazzo Campana**. Among the highlights are the **Duomo** and the **Palazzo Pretorio**. **Via delle Volte**, the medieval roadway that runs beneath the town, is like a tunnel. Colle Val d'Elsa is renowned for its glassworks whose products are exported all over the world.

Above left: 13th century city walls of Colle Val Elsa. Above right: San Gimignano. Right: Rognosa Tower on the Palazzo del Podestà.

San Gimignano of the beautiful towers

For centuries, San Gimignano has been known as the *"città delle belli torri"* (city of the beautiful towers). Of San Gimignano's fifteen surviving towerhouses, the one nicknamed *"Rognosa"* is the tallest.

Towerhouses were medieval apartment buildings. They can be regarded as the skyscrapers of the 13th and 14th centuries—they were built higher and higher as the population inside the city walls increased. By contrast, plain towers were military structures which, over the centuries, came to represent the wealth and power of the nobility. To prevent the citizenry from engaging in costly competitions, the Comune set the maximum height of buildings at 120 *braccia,* or 70 meters.

Settled by the Etruscans, San Gimignano is girthed by an unbroken circle of **city walls**. Entering by way of one of the *gates*, head for the **Fortress**, which affords a perfect view over the severe medieval configuration of the town. On your way down, before starting your tour of the monuments, wander around the little streets lined with stores where local products,

From afar, San Gimignano presents a unique cityscape of tall towerhouses. Within its walls are masterpieces by painters such as Benozzo Gozzoli; within its vats are the legendary Vernaccia wines.

including the renowned San Gimignano wines, are on sale.

There are splendid squares in San Gimignano,

foremost of which is **Piazza della Cisterna** (Square of the Well). The lovely well which gave it its name is in the middle; surrounding it are two fine towers (**Torri degli Ardinghelli**) and a palace (**Palazzo Tortoli**).

San Gimignano is a celebration and harmonious interlacing of simple, dark-hued medieval and 14th century architecture. First from a distance and then close up, observe the towers such as the **Torri dei Salvucci** and the **Torre Chigi**. There are also several works by the story-teller painter, **Benozzo Gozzoli**, including a fine *Martyrdom of St. Sebastian* in the **Duomo** and *scenes from the life of St. Sebastian* in the apse of the **church of Sant'Agostino**. Other highlights include the **Collegiata** (or **Duomo**) inside of which is the *chapel of St. Fina*, a masterpiece by **Benedetto da Maiano**, frescoed by **Ghirlandaio**. In the **Palazzo del Popolo** are two *tondos* by **Filippino Lippi**, a *Maestà* by **Lippo Memmi**, and a great *crucifix* by **Coppo di Marcovaldo**.

Above: *Piazza della Cisterna* (left) *and the* Santa Fina Chapel *by Giuliano and Benedetto da Maiano, Collegiata* (right).

And, for lunch: Vernaccia, *mushrooms,* strufoli, *and* pinolata

The cuisine in San Gimignano is Sienese, but the wine is Vernaccia *from San Gimignano. Vernaccia is one of Italy's most renowned wines, even though the production zone is a tiny forty thousand hectares. Renowned since the 13th century, it is golden in color, fragrant, and with a dry taste. It's popular as an aperitif and perfect with fish.*

Truffles and mushrooms are among the local specialties. At the end of your meal, we recommend strufoli *and* pinolata *(see page 167 for details and other desserts):* Strufoli, *a Carnival specialty, are little fried cakes made of flour, eggs, sugar, lemon, cognac and vinsanto, and coated with honey. They are so old, they have a Longobard name.* Pinolata *is a special cream and pinenut pie—that's all we intend to reveal...*

Montepulciano: the king of wines

The Renaissance enchantment of Montepulciano should not make you forget you're in one of Italy's best wine-producing centers. It's reasonable to date wine-making in the region back to the Etruscans. Incredibly, the Vino Nobile, the internationally renowned wine produced here since the 18th century, comes from only 24,000 hectares of vineyard. (See "The Wine Reports.") Here everyone knows by heart the verse penned by the 17th century scientist Francesco Redi: "Montepulciano is the king of every wine."

Above:
Montepulciano.
Right: well decorated
with griffins
and lions,
Montepulciano.

Montepulciano

Settled by the Etruscans, **Montepulciano** was first dominated by the Sienese and then by the Florentines. The quiet, sprawling hilltown is renowned for its wine. It was the birthplace of the poet Politian (b.1454-d. 1492) and the far-sighted cardinal, Bellarmino (b. 1532-d. 1621), who commissioned the town's elegant Baroque buildings. Its highlights include Renaissance architecture by Sangallo and Vignola. The heart of Montepulciano is **Piazza Grande**. The square is sur-

The solitary peacefulness of Montepulciano fills the enchanted little streets and historic squares composed of stone and overflowing with wine. The town's greatness is not only tied to a name, the poet Politian, but also to a wine, which is noble not only in name.

rounded by lovely buildings, including the **Palazzo Comunale**, which has a fine 14th century courtyard and a serenely perfect facade attributed to **Michelozzo**, the elaborate and curvilinear **Palazzo Tartugi** attributed either to **Vignola** or **Antonio da Sangallo the Elder**, and the austere **Palazzo Contucci**, which is the headquarters for one of the leading producers of *vino nobile*.

Inside the late Renaissance **Duomo** are sculptures by **Michelozzo** and a fine *triptych depicting the Assumption of the Virgin* painted by **Taddeo di Bartolo** in 1401.

Taking Via Roma, we stop at three worthy sights (**Palazzo Avignonesi**, the **church of Sant'Agostino** by **Michelozzo**, and, on Via Garibaldi, the much restored **birthplace of Politian**) on our way to the **church of San Biagio**, strikingly isolated in the countryside beyond the city walls. A Renaissance masterpiece, **San Biagio** was built by **Antonio da Sangallo the Elder** between 1518 and 1545.

Pienza

Pienza's uniqueness is reason to ponder. The town is the creation of the Humanist poet Enea Silvio Piccolomini, who was born here and who became Pope Pius II. His dream was to make the village of Corsignano into a 15th century ideal city of harmonious squares, streets, and buildings reflecting the philosophical harmony of a perfect relationship between humans and objects. Thus was born, from a 13th century family feud, the city reflecting the dreams of the Greek philosopher Plato and his Renaissance followers. The project was undertaken in 1458 by the great architect, **Bernardo Rossellino** who, influenced by his equally great contemporary, Leon Battista Alberti, designed the **Duomo**, **Palazzo Piccolomini**, the **Casa dei Canonici** (today a museum), and the **Palazzo Comunale**. Colleagues of Rossellino designed the **Palazzo Vescovile** (Bishop's Palace, formerly the Borgia Palace), **Palazzo Ammannati**, and several other buildings. Although Pius II (after whom Pienza was named) and Rossellino died before the great project could be finished, it still bears the imprint of an ideal Renaissance city.

We walk the streets of Pienza aware of how it came into being so that we can best appreciate the carefully planned spatial relationships between people and buildings and between filled and empty spaces. Among the outstanding works in the Pienza churches are an *Assumption of the Virgin* by **Vecchietta** and an *altarpiece* by **Sano di Pietro** in the **Duomo** and the *Virgin of the Misericordia* by **Signorelli** in the **church of San Francesco**. But the masterpiece of Pienza is the free air and the free sun.

Left: Caffè Poliziano, *Montepulciano.*

Below: *Pienza:* Palazzo Comunale (left) *and* Palazzo Piccolomini *by Bernardo Rossellino* (right).

Panorama of Montalcino.

Festival of the thrushes and Brunello

On the first Sunday in October, a Renaissance procession of knights and ladies, with skilled archers in the middle, winds its way to offer gifts of the earth to the "Lady of the Fortress," as the festival was called during the time of the Medici. Then, an archery contest is held in the Fortress, with fake boars as targets. All the districts of Montalcino compete for the big prize. In the evening, everyone sits down to a banquet of ham, pork, **bruschetta**, and, of course, thrushes on the spit. This is one of the rare occasions that precious Brunello flows freely. This internationally renowned wine is illustrated in "The Wine Reports."

Montalcino

Defeated by Florence in 1555, Siena attempted to revive the Republic in the fortress city of **Montalcino** (above), where the **Banner of the Sienese Republic** is still preserved. The apex of the fortress city's medieval splendor is its main **square** on which rise the **Loggia** and **Palazzo Comunale** with its stone and brick belltower and facade decorated with coats-of-arms. But it is the picturesque little streets lined with lovely buildings that endow Montalcino with its unique atmosphere. The view from the top of the fortress sweeps all the way to Siena.

After enjoying Montalcino to the hilt— walking its streets, attending its festivals, tasting its food, and, last but by no means least, drinking its legendary Brunello wine—it's a good idea to tour its cool, quiet churches and museums. Three churches, **Sant'Agostino**, **San Francesco**, and **Sant'Egidio**, are especially noteworthy. The highlights of the art museums include the *crucifix of Sant'Antimo* and 15th century carved wood statues of the *Annunciating Angel and the Virgin* by **Bartolo di Fredi** in the **Museo Diocesano** and a superb *Virgin* by di **Luca di Tommè**, a *Virgin* by **Sano di Pietro**, and *paintings* by **Bartolo di Fredi**.

Le Crete, waterless waves

Unexpectedly, seemingly out of nowhere, the striking panorama of kilometers of arid desert known as **"Le Crete"** *looms up in the midst of the harmonious verdant Sienese countryside near Asciano.* **Le Crete** *(literally, the claylands) is an area of hill-shaped clay formations that create a barren landscape of billowing waves. No vegetation grows here; only the distant shape of Monte Amiata can be made out in the background.*
After the art-packed experience of Siena, we find ourselves experiencing the spectacle of emptiness.

Above: *Chianti landscape.* Below: Castle of Meleto (left) *and* Palazzo Pretorio, *Radda in Chianti* (right).

The Sienese Chianti

The Chianti region north of Siena is one of the most beautiful in Italy. The landscape is a harmonious composition of low hills, vineyards (whose celebrated wines are discussed in "The Wine Reports"), olive groves, and cypress trees. The first town along the Via Chiantigiana is **Gaiole in Chianti**, renowned for its wines. In the environs are the **castle of Barbischio**, the fortified farm of **Meleto**, and the celebrated **castle of Brolio**, which, in the 19th century, belonged to the family of Bettino Ricasoli, the first Italian prime minister after Cavour, whose heirs are still producing the famous Ricasoli wine to-day. Continuing north, we come to Radda in Chianti, a medieval town with a fine Palazzo del Podestà and a Franciscan monastery. The last town, situated on a hilltop between the Elsa and Pesa Valleys is Castellina in Chianti, an important agricultural center.

Immersed in the scenery of the Chianti region, you'll find it hard to believe that for centuries this land was the object of constant fighting between Florence and Siena. The proof of how bitter the fighting was lies in the number of fortified castles and fortifications located on the territory. A tour of the largely intact **castles** is well worth the effort. Among the best preserved are those of **Meleto**, **Cacchiano**, and **Brolio**.

If you like old books...

In the serene and laborious quiet of the Abbazia di Monte Oliveto Maggiore is the Istituto di Patologia del Libro, world famous for its restoration of old books and for the love of culture that characterized monks and scribes over the millennium-long history of religious Italy.

Above: abbey of Monte Oliveto Maggiore: entrance (left) *and the* Great Cloister (right). Below: *San Galgano*.

In the abbeys and fortresses

Medieval Siena was not just a land of civic virtues, but, as the numerous abbeys on its territory attest, it was also imbued with mysticism and faith. Our starting point is the **church of San Galgano**, one of the masterpieces of French Cistercian Gothic architecture in Italy. Once a great center of power, it is now a picturesque ruin with the sky for a roof and grass for a floor. The church is part of the 13th century monastery complex built by the monks on the site of the 12th century hermitage of St. Galgano Guidotti. Its decline was slow, but steady. Today, the *Sala Capitolare* and the *refectory* are the only

Places for meditating: San Galgano, Abbey of Monte Oliveto, Sant'Antimo, and San Salvatore. Then, off to Monteriggioni.

parts that can be visited.

In contrast to San Galgano, the great **abbey of Monte Oliveto** has continued to flourish over the centuries. Situated thirty-three kilometers from Siena overlooking Le Crete, it was built by monks belonging to the Olivetan-Benedictine order in the 14th century. The highlights of the complex include the **church** with its remarkable carved *choirstalls*; the rectory, with old pots and pans, the huge aisled *library*, with a notable collection of rare manuscripts; and the great

Picturesque walled town of Monteriggioni.

frescoes with scenes from the life of St. Benedict by **Signorelli** and **Sodoma** in the cloister (*Chiostro Grande*). Two abbeys, **San Salvatore** and **Sant'Antimo**, are the last stops on our tour of the landmarks of Sienese mysticism. **San Salvatore**, which is also the name of the neighboring village, was founded by the Longobards in 743 and passed to the Cistercian order in the 14th century. Although the church was rebuilt in 1936, you can still visit the crypt, which dates from the original 8th century struc-

ture. The *cloister* was built in the 16th century. According to legend, the splendid Romanesque **abbey of Sant'Antimo**, built in 1118, was founded by Charlemagne. Its decline began in the 13th century. Especially noteworthy are the carved alabaster *capitals* inside the church.

The walled hilltown of **Monteriggioni** is a splendid vision from near and far. It has a splendid **church**, with a notable *baptismal font* and ruins of a *cloister*. Yet the whole is somehow greater than the sum of its parts.

Chianciano: miraculous waters

Situated in verdant parklands, the spa of Chianciano has since the time of the Etruscans and Romans been renowned for its calcium-sulfate mineral waters that help to cure liver problems and digestive diseases. A two-kilometer long tree-shaded avenue connects the old town to the internationally known modern spa, which has facilities for sports, including a swimming pool. In the old town are Etruscan ruins, an 18th century **fountain***, a splendid* **Collegiata Church***, and the 13th century* **Palazzo del Podestà***.*

Etruscan and Roman before becoming a free commune, Arezzo has historically been a prosperous agricultural center and the birthplace of great artists such as Piero della Francesca and Giorgio Vasari, whose masterpieces can still be admired in the city and the environs. Today, Arezzo is renowned as an antiques and jewelry-producing center.

AREZZO

From the Etruscans to gold

Arezzo's history goes back to the Etruria. One of the major Etruscan cities, it became an important Roman city, celebrated for its foundries and vases known as **"vasi corallini"** (whose innovative manufacturing technique spread throughout the Roman Empire). In the Middle Ages, Arezzo was a Ghibelline free commune: It was defeated by Guelph Florence in the celebrated battle of Campaldino fought in 1289. Later, subjugated to Florence, it was annexed to the Grandduchy of Tuscany. In more modern times, it has been a major agricultural center. After World War II, it became a manufacturing city, specializing in textiles and jewelry.

Arezzo is a compendium of masterpieces from every period of Italian art: from Etruscan and Roman (Roman **amphitheater** and the celebrated **Chimera**, now on display in the Florence Museo Archeologico, but originally excavated in Arezzo), late medieval (**Cimabue's** *crucifix* in the **church of San Domenico**), Gothic (**church of San Francesco**, the **Palazzo Pretorio**, and the **Palazzo Comunale**), Renaissance (including **Piero della Francesca's** *frescoes* in **San Francesco**, **Benedetto da Maiano's** *portico* of the **church of Santa Maria delle Grazie**, **Antonio da Sangallo's Fortress**, and *sculp-*

Facing page: *Sansepolcro:* Resurrection of Christ *by Piero della Francesca* (detail), Museo Civico (above) *and Piazza Grande* (below).

This page: *Arezzo:* Duomo (below) *and* Santa Maria delle Grazia *with a porch by Benedetto da Maiano* (bottom).

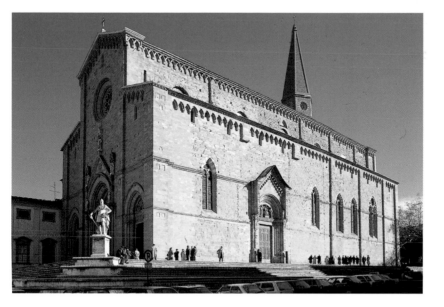

The Golden Legend

Arezzo is a major gold-working center, transforming ten percent of the world's newly mined gold and forty percent of the gold worked in Italy into marvels of jewelry, medals, and objets d'art. Currently, there are over seventy industries and 450 artisans involved in

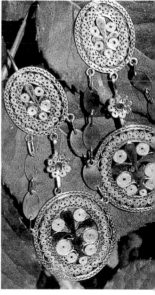

ture by **Bernardo Rossellino**), Baroque (**Palazzo del Tribunale** and **Santissima Trinità**), to neo-Classic (**Teatro Petrarca**). Arezzo was also the birthplace of author-artist **Giorgio Vasari**, whose house has been preserved as a museum.

Arezzo is not just a city of art of the past, but it also ranks as a major industrial center. From time immemorial, its town meeting-place has been the impressive square, **Piazza Grande**, adorned with a fine well. The square hosts two major event: the great open-air *antiques fair*, held monthly, and the *Giostra del Saracino* (Saracen Tournament), held in September.

Pleasantly situated on the slopes of a hill, Arezzo is crossed by three major thoroughfares, each leading to one of its principal regions: the Valdichiana, the Valdarno, and the Casentino. After Piazza Grande, our rapid walking tour proceeds to **Piazza Guido Monaco**, on which stands a *monument to*

gold working in the city. The largest and best known is Gori-Zucchi's Uno-A-Erre, which was been operating since 1926. Arezzo's goldwork is renowned for its high technology and high quality.

St. Francis *by Margarito d'Arezzo, Museo Statale d'Arte (13th century).*

Crucifix *by Cimabue, San Domenico (13th century).*

Tomb of St. Donato, *main altar of the* Duomo *(14th century).*

Guido Monaco, the Aretine who invented musical notes, and then on to **Piazza del Duomo**. Inside the **Duomo**, with its magnificent stained-glass windows, is the 14th century *Cappella Tarlati* and, next to the sacristy, **Piero della Francesca's** *fresco of Mary Magdalene*.

Foremost among Arezzo's churches is **San Francesco**, with a plain, unfinished facade, inside of which is **Piero della Francesca's** peerless fresco cycle recounting the *Legend of the True Cross*. Other great churches are the **Pieve of Santa Maria**, whose Romanesque apse can be admired from Piazza Grande and whose exterior is adorned with blind arcading, loggias, and portals, and the **church of Santa Maria delle Grazie**, with a remarkable external *loggia* supported by Corinthian columns by **Benedetto da Maiano** and a fine *main altar* by Andrea della Robbia.

Arezzo is full of marvelous palaces. Two of the most famous are situated in Piazza Grande: the **Palazzo della Fraternita dei Laici**, a 15th century building designed by **Bernardo Rossellino** and the sumptuous **Palazzo delle Logge**, designed by **Vasari**. Noteworthy buildings, many of which still flanked by protective towers, are located on the town's main street, Corso Italia. Nearby is the elegant medieval building, **Palazzo Pretorio**.

There are two other sights of historical interest that you shouldn't miss: the **birthplace of the poet Petrarch**, which is now a foundation (*Accademia Petrarca di Lettere, Arti e Scienze*) and the **birthplace of author-artist Giorgio Vasari**, which is now a **museum**.
You get a magnificent view from the **Fortezza Medicea**, an elegant military complex designed by **Giuliano** and **Antonio da Sangal-**

One fair, many antiques dealers

The young-at-heart antiques

Arezzo is the capital of antiques. Since 1968, on the first Sunday of each month, it has hosted an immense antiques show that, from **Piazza Grande**, spills into the surrounding medieval streets. Thousands upon thousands of antiques from Italy and abroad are on sale. The select pieces of every kind and description are guaranteed genuine. In keeping with its tradition as an art and antiques center, Arezzo also has numerous art galleries and antiques shops that make it a trendsetter in Italy's art market quotations.

Noble folklore in Arezzo

The Giostra del Saracino (Saracen Tournament)

The **Giostra del Saracino** (Saracen Tournament) is held the first Sunday in September in **Piazza di San Domenico**. Supposedly, it goes back to the 13th century, when Dante himself is said to have attended the games. It is preceded by a splendid historic procession. Each of the competing teams represent one of the four districts of the city. The object of the game is for the players, mounted and carrying lances, to hit a shield bearing a moving image of the enemy, Buratto. The winner receives a golden lance and his district celebrates by throwing a huge party.

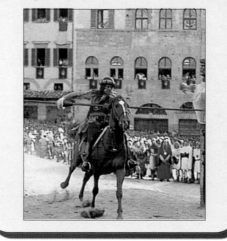

Facing page: Palazzo Comunale (above), Palazzo Pretorio (center), *and* San Francesco *frescoed by Piero della Francesca* (below).

lo in the 16th century. In addition to great architecture and masterpieces of painting, Arezzo has two important museums: the **Museo Archeologico Mecenate** and the **Museo Nazionale Moderno**.
Prehistoric, Etruscan and Roman pieces, as well as a precious collection of the typical Aretine vases known as *"vasi corallini"* are displayed in the **Museo Archeologico Mecenate**, which is housed in the 16th century monastery of San Bernardo. In the **Museo Nazionale Moderno**, housed in a 15th century palace attributed to Bernardo Rossellino, are Italian paintings and sculpture, mostly of the Tuscan school, and a rare collection of majolica ceramics. Among the prominent artists represented are **Luca Signorelli**, **Rosso Fiorentino**, **Bernardo Rossellino** and **Vasari**, as well as **Giovanni Fattori** and **Telemaco Signorini**, two of the major figures of the 19th century Tuscan **Macchiaioli** school.

The chestnut kingdom

Chestnuts and firs make up the medieval forests of Camaldoli and Vallombrosa that cover the slopes of the Casentino region. Chestnuts have been a staple of country food for centuries. Poor folk used them in every way: they boiled and roasted them; they ground them into flour and made them into delicious desserts such as **casta-gnaccio** or chestnut cakes. Today, however, as people and their diets have become richer, chestnuts now represent only a marginal food of their diet. For more details about chestnuts, see "The Chestnut Report."

The ancient, solitary, mystical beauty of the land of

CASENTINO

amid hermits and sanctuaries, woodlands, old legends, and country cooking

Above: *panoramic view over the Casentino region with the castle of Poppi in the background.* Center: *Piazza Tanucci, Stia.* Below: *Badia Prataglia and the* Parco Nazionale delle Foreste Casentinesi.

The **Casentino** region lies between Florence and Arezzo in the Arno Valley, covering the territory of what was the fiefdom of the Guidi Counts. Covered with thick forests (now the Parco Nazionale delle Foreste Casentinesi), it is a lonely region, prone to mysticism. Its main attraction, in addition to nature, are its *pievi* (country churches, which were complexes each of which had its own baptistery and cemetery) and castles. Most of them were built by the Benedictine order in the transitional style between Romanesque and Gothic. The most famous are those of **Romena**, **Stia**, **Montemignaio**, **Socana**, and **Ristonchi**. The *pievi*, which were of vast political importance throughout the Middle Ages, were built along the main roads that crossed the great valleys.

By contrast, the **castles** were built on hilltops. Among the most famous are those of

(continued on page 182)

Two stopovers for the spirit

La Verna and Camaldoli: two holy places in Tuscany

The **hermitage of Camaldoli** (above) combines spiritual and physical beauty. It rises amid a forest of chestnuts, firs, and oaks, where titmice and woodpeckers make their nests and primroses and snowdrops burst into flower. Towering above the rest is the **Miraglia Chestnut**, a gigantic, thousand-year-old tree whose hollow trunk is big enough to hold a table. The land on which the complex rises was donated to the monks by a wealthy merchant, Maldolo. For this reason, it was known as **"casa di Maldolo,"** then **"ca' Maldolo,"** and finally **"Camaldoli."** St. Romualdo founded the **monastery**, with its little cell-houses inside of which the monks lived and prayed. The picturesque **pharmacy**, dating from 1543, offers products from the distillation of plants and medicinal herbs such as valerian, stramonium, henbane, lime, and mint. (See "The Monastery Report.")

The **sanctuary of La Verna** (below), is situated 1100 meters above sea level in the middle of a forest. It was built in 1213 on the site of the monastery founded by St. Francis, who later received the stigmata in La Verna. The monastery complex includes the **Chiesa Maggiore** (Greater Church) and the **Chiesetta di Santa Maria degli Angeli** (Little Church of St. Mary of the Angels), along with five cloisters and the grotto inhabited by St. Francis. Noteworthy are the **chapel of the Stigmata** and the glazed terracottas by **Andrea** and **Luca Della Robbia**.

Pieve di Romena

The **Pieve di Romena**, the most famous of the Casentino pievi, was built in 1152. A masterpiece of Romanesque architecture, it bears the strong imprint of the Cistercian style, which at the time was prevalent in France and Germany. It has a striking plain stone facade with a flanking belltower. Inside the single-aisled church are stupendous carved capitals decorated with foliage and symbolic motifs.

Dante at Campaldino

A few kilometers from the town of Ponte a Poppi, at the intersection for Stia and Pontassieve, you will see a column rising in the countryside with the coats-of-arms of Arezzo and Florence. It was built to remind travelers that they are in the plain of Campaldino where, in June 1289, Arezzo was defeated by Florence at the battle of Campaldino. Among the Florentine troops was Dante Alighieri, who mentions the historic battle several times in The Divine Comedy.

Poppi, which once belonged to the Guidi Counts, **Chiusi della Verna**, **Subbiano**, and **Porciano**. Towns protected by the castles sprung up in their environs. Aside from the hermitages of Camaldoli and La Verna, the towns of the Casentino region originated as noble castles. We shall touch on **Capolona**, **Subbiano**, **Talla**, **Montemignaio**, **Badia Prataglia**, elegant **Stia**, and the foremost of the walled castles, **Poppi**.

The **castle of Poppi** is a must: It has a superb *library*, magnificent rooms, and architecture by Arnolfo di Cambio.

Above: *panoramic view of Poppi with a close-up of the castle* (insert).

Traditional Casentino cooking

Try scottiglia!

The legendary dish of the Casentino, **scottiglia**, is a meat **cacciucco**, or meat stew, made of beef, pork, chicken, pigeon, and duck, boiled for hours in a broth flavored with tomato, red wine, and chili pepper. It presumably originated in the area around Monte Falterona in the Middle Ages. It's a tasty, if not digestible, dish. According to food historians, it is possible that the renowned **acquacotta grossetano** originated in the Casentino region, which is celebrated for its genuine foods and culinary genius. Seasonal specialties include grugiate (roast chestnuts) and snails, which have been considered a delicacy since Antiquity. According to the Casentino recipe, the snails are cooked for two hours in a spicy meat sauce. During Easter a popular treat is the special bread flavored with spices and raisins known as "**panina**" or "**panina gialla**" (yellow bread with saffron). "**Sbriciolona**," flavored with fennel seeds, is the softer version of the Tuscan salami known as "**finocchiona**".

Porta Fiorentina
(Florentine Gate),
Castelfranco di Sopra
(far left) *and* Museo
Paleontologico,
Montevarchi (left).

VALDARNO

Opulent and full of grace, the Valdarno region is alive with color from the juxtaposition of belltowers, pievi, oak forests, and olive groves

Valdarno (literally, Valley of the Arno) as the upper valley of the Arno is called, is lovely in the harmonious Tuscan manner. Like the rest of the region, it is a combination of wonders of art and natur.

San Giovanni Valdarno, **Castelfranco di Sopra**, and **Terranova Bracciolini** are the survivors of what were originally a group of seven fortified towns. They were designed at the end the 13th century by the architect, Arnolfo di Cambio, who was commissioned by the **Signoria** governers of Florence to build *"terre murate,"* i.e., walled towns, in the Valdarno. As a result, all the towns share the same configuration: Rectangular in shape, they have a central square, parallel and perpendicular streets, and walls with bastions.

San Giovanni Valdarno has several noteworthy sights, including the **Palazzo Comunale** designed by **Arnolfo di Cambio**, the basilica of Santa Maria delle Grazie, and the Gothic **church of San Lorenzo**, which has some lovely frescoes. Take time to tour **Montevarchi**, originally the Guidi Counts' castle and today at thriving agricultural market and producer of woven garments and shoes. Among the sights are the **Collegiata of San Lorenzo** and the **Museo Paleontologico**, with displays regarding the animals who roamed the Valdarno in the Pliocene era.

Gropina of the extraordinary capitals

Gropina, one of the finest of the Casentino **pievi**, rises in the area near Loro Ciuffenna. Originally built in the 8th century, it was later remodeled as we see it today: a simple stone building flanked by a belltower. Inside are extraordinary 12th century **carved capitals** (below) in which foliage patterns and animal and human figures are intertwined in complex symbolism.

The sublime realism of the *Madonna del Parto* of Monterchi

Monterchi, thirty kilometers from Arezzo, is the birthplace of Piero della Francesca's mother where there has always been a tradition of popular devotion to the Virgin, protectress of maternity. For centuries, art-lovers have made the pilgrimage to see the fresco of the **Madonna del Parto** (Virgin of Childbirth) which Piero painted in 1450. The majestic Renaissance beauty of the Virgin overshadows the daring realism of the garment slightly open on her swollen belly with her hand posed it in the typical manner of a pregnant woman.

Two views of the Valtiberina: Monterchi (above) *and Anghiari* (right).

VALTIBERINA

The Valtiberina region is characterized by stunning variety of customs and landscapes. It is the birthplace of Piero della Francesca, many of whose masterpieces may still be admired here, and of Michelangelo.

The Valtiberina region, named for the valley of the Tiber River flowing through it, is the easternmost part of Tuscany. Here, in Antiquity, Romans erected villas, and, in the Middle Ages, bishops and abbeys built monasteries and powerful families built castles. It was also the birthplace of two of Italy's sublime artistic geniuses: Piero della Francesca and Michelangelo.

As you tour Valtiberina, keep your eyes out for the combined influence that the neighboring regions of Romagna, Marche, and Umbria had on its language, customs, arts and crafts, and architecture. We shall only touch upon the highlights: the tiny town of **Monterchi**, where you can admire Piero della Francesca's **Madonna del Parto**; **Anghiari**, enclosed inside a girth of medieval walls; **Sansepolcro**, foremost of the Valtiberina cities, and lastly, the stupendous Renaissance town of **Cortona**.

The feud of Anghiari goes back to 1082. Until 1440, it belonged to the Camaldolesi monks and their

priors and thereafter, although it sided with Arezzo, it fell under Florentine domination. The highlights of the town are the old **city walls**, the 17th century **church of Santa Maria delle Grazie**, the medieval **church of Badia**, the Renaissance **Palazzo Taglieschi**, and the **Museo Statale delle Arti e Tradizioni Popolari dell'Alta Valle del Tevere**. A few kilometers from Anghieri is the newly restored **Pieve di Sovara**, a fine example of the Romanesque style.

Sansepolcro, a busy industrial center, is the site of the historic "**Palio della Balestra**," a contest in medieval costume held on the second Sunday in September. Even more importantly, it is the birthplace of the great Early Renaissance painter **Piero della Francesca** (whose works, mostly preserved in the **Museo Civico**, are illustrated on page 186). In addition to the works of Piero della Francesca, the highlights of Sansepolcro are the 11th century **Duomo**, the **Palazzo delle Laudi**, with its lovely courtyard, and

Polenta Festival

Every fourth Sunday in September, Monterchi hosts a food festival featuring **polenta** (cornmeal), sausages, and pigs' livers, which is well attended by tourists and gourmets. It is the perfect occasion for the historic town to celebrate its heritage with dancing, singing, and good food.

the **Palazzo Pretorio**, whose facade is adorned with coats-of-arms. Sansepolcro is a fascinating example of a medieval town with fine Renaissance and Baroque buildings.

In touring the Valtiberina region, don't miss the Romanesque **Pieve Santo Stefano**, with its two medieval palaces, the **Palazzo Comunale** and the **Palazzo Pretorio**. Sestino, a delightful little mountain town, is famous for two reasons: It has an interesting **archeological museum** (with a fine headless Venus dating from the Roman period) and the local *truffles* are superb.

Caprese Michelangelo: Michelangelo's birthplace

First mentioned in 11th century documents, Caprese Michelangelo was subjugated first by Arezzo and then, in the late 1200s, by Florence, who sent a Podestà *(governor) to rule over it. Its medieval walls have come down to us intact. Michelangelo Buonarroti, the son of the* Podestà *then in service, was born on March 6, 1475 in the* Casa del Podestà, *i.e., the governor's official residence. Today, the rustic building with its external staircase is the* Museo Michelangiolesco, *which displays life-size reproductions of the master's works, as well as contemporary sculpture.*

Perspective becomes poetry

The masterpieces by Piero della Francesca alone are worth a visit to Tuscany. The perspective that he perfected became the rational principle for investigating the natural world around him; his timeless crystalline universe was born from his studies of geometry applied to reality. Influenced by the Flemish painters, he in turn influenced Venetian art, as well as Raphael and Bramante in Rome. His looming figures exude a sense of monumentality and the eternal, for many unsurpassed in Western art. Most of Piero's works can still be seen in Tuscany. His first work is the **Altarpiece of the Misericordia** in **Sansepolcro**, where the figure of the Virgin welcomes and shelters the faithful beneath her protective cloak. Even more famous

Piero della Francesca: scenes from the Legend of the True Cross, *San Francesco, Arezzo* (above) *and* Madonna del Parto, *Monterchi* (right).

is the **Madonna del Parto** (Virgin of Childbirth), painted for the chapel in the Monterchi cemetery, which is a rare depiction of the Mother of Christ as a pregnant woman about to give birth. Another monumental figure is that of the Christ in the geometrically constructed Resurrection painted between 1463 and 1465. Perhaps his most impressive feat, however, is the fresco cycle of the **Legend of the True Cross** in the **church of San Francesco** in Arezzo. The popular medieval legend recounts how the cross on which Christ was crucified was discovered, pilfered, and then returned to Jerusalem.

Like his great predecessors, Giotto and Masaccio, and like his great descendent, Michelangelo, Piero represents a universal milestone in art history.

Piero della Francesca: Resurrection of Christ (above) *and the* Altarpiece of Mercy, (left), *both in the* Museo Civico, *Sansepolcro.*

VALDICHIANA

The Valdichiana region, with its delightful scenery and charming towns, is full of art treasures ranging from Etruscan tomb fittings to paintings by Luca Signorelli.

Lucignano

A walk around the unusual elliptical-shaped town of **Lucignano** is soothing to the spirit. The main thoroughfare that winds concentrically around the hillside leads up to the 17th century **Collegiata** church. In the **Museo Civico** is another treasure, the celebrated **Tree of the Cross**, a precious reliquary in gold, crafted in Siena in the 14th century.

The tranquil landscape of the **Valdichiana** region, the largest of the Apennine valleys, at the same time conceals and reveals the events of its two-thousand-year-old history. Once the granary of Etruria (Etruscan remains can be found in **Camucia**, **Sodo**, and **Foiano**), by the Middle Ages it had become an immense marshland—which is how Leonardo depicted it in his notebooks *(Atlantic Codex)*. In the 19th century, under the Granddukes of Tuscany, the marshes were drained and many architecturally interesting rural structures were built. (See "The Farmhouse Report.")

The sights in the region include towns such as **Castiglion Fiorentino** (with the fine **castle of Montecchio**), **Foiano della Chiana**, the elliptical-shaped **Lucignano**, and **Cortona**, the birthplace of three of the great Renaissance masters: Luca Signorelli, Andrea Sansovino, and Pietro da Cortona.

Above: *aerial view of Lucignano* (left) *and the* castle of Montecchio, *Castiglion Fiorentino* (right). Right: *panoramic view of Castiglion Fiorentino.*

CORTONA

The remarkable Etruscan lamp, the Flagellation *by Luca Signorelli, the harmony of* Santa Maria delle Grazie *in Calcinaio: highlights of a lovely land.*

Whipped by the wind that renders smooth its *pietra serena* buildings, Cortona is perched on a hilltop waiting to show off its charming little streets, Medici fortress, and imposing Etruscan walls.

Cortona is a treasure trove of art, with works of Etruscan monumentality standing alongside works representing the most refined Humanism of the Italian Renaissance. Foremost among the Etruscan pieces is the incredible decorated *bronze lamp*, probably dating from the 5th century B.C. displayed in the **Museo dell'Accademia Etrusca**. Paintings of the *Lamentation*, the *Last Supper*, and the *Flagellation of Christ* by native by **Luca Signorelli** are displayed in the **Museo Dioccsano**. The treatment of the figures exhibits the Florentine linear dynamism that would inspire Michelangelo.

Above: *Cortona, a detail of the* Virgin and Child with Saints *by Luca Signorelli*, Museo dell'Accademia Etrusca *(1523).* Below: theater *in Piazza Signorelli* (left) *and* hermitage of Celle *founded by St. Francis* (right).

Here you don't just look at antiques— you buy'em

Arezzo and its environs are where the Italians' love for their heritage is translated into the preservation of antiques. Like Arezzo, Cortona holds a monthly antiques fair and other events that draw a highly qualified of antiques dealers and experts. In addition to the bric-a-brac available all over Italy, you can find quality paintings, *objets d'art*, and furniture.

Above: Santa Maria delle Grazie *by Francesco di Giorgio Martini, Calcinaio.* Center: Last Supper *by Luca Signorelli (predella of the* Lamentation of Christ*), Museo Diocesano, Cortona.*

Other highlights of Cortona are the **church of San Francesco** (with a fine Byzantine reliquary) and the **church of San Niccolò**, the **sanctuary of St. Margherita** (with a superb facade and the 14th century tomb of the saint), and the **hermitage of the Celle** founded by St. Francis. Leave time for a brief excursion to the remarkable Renaissance **church of Santa Maria delle Grazie** by **Francesco di Giorgio Martini**, which is located at Calcinaio (three kilometers) and the nearby **abbey of Farneta**.

The best quality meats from the Valdichiana pastures

The cows that give the best meat, the **chianina** *breed, are raised in the Valdichiana for the famous* "**bistecca alla fiorentina**" *(Florentine steak) Maybe it's due to the air, or to the pastures, or to the special characteristics of the* **chianina** *breed—whatever the reason may be, the* **chianina** *steak is reputed the best in Tuscany. Florentines are traditionally big consumers of meat. Giovanni Villani wrote in his* Cronica *(Chronicles) in the late 1300s that the Florentines consumed "approximately four thousand cows and calves and thirty thousand pigs in a year." In addition to steak (which will be discussed in greater detail in the section on Florence), other popular Tuscan dishes made from* **chianina** *cows are tripe, offal, and kidneys.*

INDEX

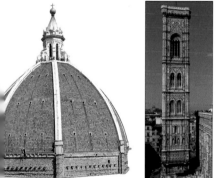